MOTOR LEARNING
IN CHILDHOOD EDUCATION

ABOUT THE AUTHOR

James H. Humphrey, Professor Emeritus at the University of Maryland, has been considered an eminent authority on child development and learning for over three decades. He has published over 60 books which have been adopted for use in over 1,200 colleges and universities. He has also written 13 children's books and created four educational record albums. In addition, his 200 articles and research reports have appeared in over 20 different national and international journals. Dr. Humphrey has received numerous educational honors and awards and has been a distinguished visiting professor in four universities.

MOTOR LEARNING
IN CHILDHOOD EDUCATION
Curricular • Compensatory • Cognitive

By

JAMES H. HUMPHREY, ED.D.
Professor Emeritus
University of Maryland

CHARLES C THOMAS • PUBLISHER
Springfield • Illinois • U.S.A.

Published and Distributed Throughout the World by

CHARLES C THOMAS • PUBLISHER
2600 South First Street
Springfield, Illinois 62794-9265

© *1992 by* CHARLES C THOMAS • PUBLISHER

ISBN 0-398-05795-8

Library of Congress Catalog Card Number: 92-3471

Printed in the United States of America
SC-R-3

Library of Congress Cataloging-in-Publication Data

Humphrey, James Harry, 1911–
    Motor learning in childhood education : curricular, compensatory.
cognitive / by James H. Humphrey.
        p.   cm.
    Includes bibliographical references (p.   ) and index.
    ISBN 0-398-05795-8 (cloth)
    1. Perceptual-motor learning.   2. Education, Elementary.
I. Title.
LB1067.H86   1992
155.4'123—dc20   92-3471
                                                                              CIP

INTRODUCTION

Over a period of years the term *motor learning* has been defined in a number of ways. Most of these definitions are more alike than they are different, tending to center around the general idea that motor learning is concerned only with the learning of motor skills. As an example, over two decades ago the *Dictionary of Education* differentiated between what might be termed *ideational* learning and *motor* learning in the following manner: Ideational learning is concerned with ideas, concepts, and mental associations, while motor learning is that in which the learner achieves new facility in the performance of bodily movements as a result of specific practice.[1]

Although this may have been a convenient and simple description of motor learning, it did not serve the purpose adequately. The reason for this being that motor learning could no longer be considered a unilateral entity. At one time when thought of only in terms of learning motor skills, it might have been considered by some as almost the exclusive purview of the physical educator and psychologist. However it soon became such a multiphasic area that it compelled the interest and attention of a variety of professions and disciplines. In fact, in modern times in almost any endeavor of human concern that one might mention, some aspect of motor learning could play a very significant part. For this reason it becomes evident that we should no longer think of motor learning only in the sense of the previously mentioned definition. Consequently, some attempt needed to be made to identify certain branches of specific aspects of motor learning.

In the late 1960s in order to put it into its proper perspective, I identified three specific aspects of motor learning. It should be understood that these identifications were used arbitrarily for my own purpose. Perhaps others might choose to identify these differently, and in the absence of anything resembling standardized terminology, it would cer-

---

[1]Good, Carter V., *Dictionary of Education*, 2nd edition, New York, McGraw-Hill, p. 314, 1959.

tainly be their prerogative to do so. Moreover, it is also recognized that some individuals might wish to segment these aspects of motor learning further, or add others. With this idea in mind I have identified the three aforementioned aspects as follows:

1. Motor learning which is concerned essentially with conditions surrounding the *learning of motor skills.* This was later expanded to include curriculum content in which the motor skills could be applied, and was identified as *curricular motor learning.*
2. Motor learning which is concerned essentially with *perceptual motor development.* This may also be referred to as *psychomotor development* or *neuromotor perceptual training.* This was identified as *compensatory motor learning.*
3. Motor learning which is concerned essentially with *academic skill and concept development.* This was identified as *cognitive motor learning.*

It should be clearly understood that all of the above areas of motor learning involve the same general basic concept; and that there are various degrees of interrelatedness and interdependence of each area upon the other.

The book is organized into three parts: curricular motor learning, compensatory motor learning, and cognitive motor learning.

Part I is concerned with a discussion of curricular motor learning, learning of motor skills and curriculum content in which these motor skills can be applied.

Part II starts with an overview of compensatory motor learning and takes into account how motor learning experiences can be utilized to improve upon such qualities as body awareness, laterality and directionaly, visual and auditory perception, and kinesthetic and tactile perception.

In Part III the concept of cognitive motor learning is discussed in detail along with how motor learning is concerned with the development of skills and concepts in the elementary school curriculum areas of reading, mathematics, and science.

CONTENTS

vii

MOTOR LEARNING
IN CHILDHOOD EDUCATION

PART I
CURRICULAR MOTOR LEARNING

Chapter 1

OVERVIEW

Curricular motor learning has commanded the attention of individuals in the field of physical education mainly because it forms the basic citadel for subject matter and methods of teaching in this field. Some of the areas in which attention has been centered include: how individuals learn motor skills, length and distribution of practice, mechanical principles, transfer, and retention. Research in some of these areas by some physical educators has been outstanding, and as might be expected it has been done primarily by those who have a background in psychology.

Over the years it appears that there has been more compatibility between psychologists and physical educators regarding this branch of motor learning. The fact that such was not always the case is suggested in the following comment over three decades ago by one psychologist:[1] "There is one perhaps distressing feature which is apparent: this is the seeming lack of awareness which the two disciplines have of the progress *and* problems of the other's area."

Fortunately, over time there has been evidence of amelioration of this condition because more and more, psychologists have discovered that physical education and sports experiences provide an excellent natural climate and laboratory for the study of human performance and behavior.

Since curricular motor learning is the basis for subject matter and methods of teaching in physical education, we need to focus on physical education as a subject in the elementary school curriculum.

Physical education should be a curriculum area in the elementary school curriculum in the same manner as mathematics is a curriculum area, or science is a curriculum area, and so on. Such factors as sufficient facilities, adequate time allotment, and above all, good teaching, should be provided to carry out the most desirable physical education learning experiences for children. A curriculum that is child-oriented and scien-

---

[1]Johnson, G. B., Motor learning. In W. R. Johnson, *Science and Medicine in Exercise and Sports*, New York, Harper and Brothers, p. 602, 1960.

tifically developed should be provided as would be the case with the language arts curriculum or the social studies curriculum or any other curriculum in the elementary school. The child should learn to move efficiently and effectively and to learn the various kinds of motor skills. This should include the locomotor skills, auxiliary skills, and skills of propulsion and retrieval needed for satisfactory performance in active games, rhythmic activities, and self-testing activities.

HISTORICAL DEVELOPMENT AND CURRENT TRENDS

In order to present a clearer picture of the place of physical education in the modern elementary school, it seems appropriate to discuss briefly its past development. Moreover, if we can see how the past has challenged the present, there is a strong likelihood that we may be able to understand more fully how the present might challenge the future.

There is a widespread notion among some people that physical education at the elementary school level is something new. This idea is probably prompted by the fact that physical education at this level keeps receiving more attention and the additional fact that more emphasis is being put on it in some school systems.

Physical education at the elementary school level is not of recent origin. In fact, educators and philosophers as far back as the early Greeks felt that physical education activities might be a welcome adjunct to the total education of children. For instance, over 2,300 years ago Plato suggested that all early education should be a sort of play and develop around play situations.

In the 17th century, Locke, the English philosopher, felt that children should get plenty of exercise and learn to swim early in life. Rousseau, the notable French writer, held much the same opinion, believing that learning should develop from the activities of childhood. These men, along with numerous others, influenced to some extent the path that elementary school physical education was to follow through the years.

Throughout the ages physical education programs have been caught between mere preparation for combat and a recognition of the essential unity of the mind and body in the educative process. In addition, there have been periods when any type of physical education program was abandoned purely on the basis that body pleasure of any sort must be subjugated because it was associated with evil doing. The early American pioneers more or less typified this kind of puritannical thinking because there was no emphasis on physical education for the pioneer child as far as formal education was concerned. Although physical education received no attention in the early American schools, a series of factors over a period of a few years were instrumental in effecting a radical change, such as Western expansion, wars, application of inventions which revolutionized travel and communications, and the concentration of population, all having an influence on the growth of the early common schools. Although the early grade schools of the mid-19th century were concerned predominantly with the academic subject matter of reading, writing, and arithmetic, the need for physical activity as a part of the school day was becoming evident. As a result, some time for physical exercise was alloted in the school programs of Boston as early as 1852. St. Louis and Cincinnati followed this procedure in 1855 and 1859 respectively. Interest at the state level began to appear and a state law requiring physical education was passed in California in 1866. The fact that the public was becoming conscious of the play needs of children was indicated by the establishment of the first playground in Boston in 1885.

In 1889 in that same city an interesting development occurred at a "conference in the interest of physical training." Some school administrators were beginning to feel the pressure and need for some kind of formal physical activity as a genuine part of the school program. Acting in a conservative manner at this conference, some school administrators proposed that a "physical training" program might be introduced as a part of the school day, but that it must consume only a short period of time, minimal expenditure of money, and take place in the classroom. The Swedish pedogogical system of gymnastics, which was designed to systematically exercise the entire body in a single lesson, was proposed since this system satisfactorily met the criteria established by the school administrators. On June 24, 1890, the Boston School Committee voted that this system of gymnastics be introduced in all of the public schools of Boston. Although this proposal was a far cry from a well-balanced elementary school physical education program as we understand it today, it nevertheless served as a formal introduction of organized physical activity into the elementary school on the recommendation of school administrators. It should be mentioned, however, that the main objective of physical education in the eyes of school administrators of that day was that it should serve as a release for prolonged periods of mental fatigue. It was believed that the main purpose of engaging in physical activity was to provide children with a "break" in the school day so that they would approach their studies more vigorously.

This condition existed until such time that there was more widespread acceptance of the theory of mind-body relationship and the education of the *whole* person. John Dewey, one of the early believers in this principle, introduced the concept of a balanced physical education program while at the University of Chicago Laboratory School early in this century. Rather than the more or less formalized gymnastics program, this school began to include games and dancing as a part of the physical education experiences of children. Some years later Dewey commented that "Experience has shown that when children have a chance at physical activities which bring their natural impulses into play, going to school is a joy, management is less of a burden, and learning is easier.[2]

However, up until the First World War physical education programs for elementary school children, where they did exist, consisted mainly of the formalized gymnastics and/or exercise types of programs. The period between the two world wars saw more attempts at balancing physical education programs at the elementary school level with more emphasis being placed upon games and rhythmic activities.

After World War II a number of factors developed which were to bring attention to the importance of physical education for young children. One estimate indicated that from the period of 1945 to 1955 more published material appeared relating to elementary school physical education than was the case in the preceding 50 years. In addition, many areas of the country began to provide elementary school physical education workshops and other in-service devices for elementary school personnel. In 1948, at its annual convention, the American Association for Health, Physical Education and Recreation inaugurated an Elementary School Physical Education Section with the present author as its first chairman-elect. And in 1951 the first National Conference on Physical Education for Children of Elementary School Age was held in Washington, D.C. (The term *Association* has been changed to *Alliance* in this national organization.)

The period from 1950 to 1975 saw a continuation of the foundation that had been laid in the preceding years. Numerous national conferences, the appointment of an Elementary School Consultant by the Alliance,

---

[2]Dewey, John, *Democracy and Education, An Introduction to Philosophy of Education*. New York, Macmillan. 1919, pp. 228–229.

and upgrading of teacher preparation in the area of elementary school physical education have been important factors. The "discovery" of the importance of *movement* in the lives of children has contributed to better elementary school physical education programs in the decade of the 1980 and until the present time.

With regard to movement, it seems appropriate at this point to comment on what has been called *movement education.* It is the belief of most physical educators that *movement* is the term which is most characteristic of the body of knowledge and subject matter in physical education. A common description of movement, when it is applied to human beings, is muscular action involving a change in body position. The human organism interacts with its environment through changes in the position of the body and/or its segments through movement.

It is difficult to fix an exact date when the term *movement education* was introduced into the United States. However, it appears that this area was beginning to become known in this country in the mid-1950s, although it was a few years later before there was much widespread interest in it in elementary schools. Many people feel that movement education originated in England but there are some who contend that the way that it has been conducted is a product of the thinking of American physical educators.

One of the problems encountered in movement education has been the difficulty of understanding its meaning. So many different definitions of it have been set forth in the literature that widespread confusion about the meaning of it has resulted.

Perhaps a generalized view would describe it as the *development of total human potential.* In movement education this is said to be accomplished by giving children freedom to explore various forms of movement with reference to such qualities as *time, force, space,* and *flow.* A brief comment on each of these qualities follows.

1. *Time.* Time is concerned with how long it takes to complete a movement. For example, a movement can be slow and deliberate such as a child attempting to create his own body movement to depict a falling snowflake. On the other hand, a movement might be made with sudden quickness such as starting to run for a goal on a signal.
2. *Force.* Force needs to be applied to set the body or one of its segments in motion as well as to change its speed and/or direction.

Thus, force is concerned with how much strength is required for movement. Swinging an arm requires less strength than attempting to propel the body over the surface area with a standing broad jump.

3. *Space.* In general, there are two factors concerned with space. These are the amount of space required to perform a particular movement and the utilization of space available.

4. *Flow.* All movements involve some degree of rhythm in their performance; thus, flow is concerned with the sequence of movement involving rhythmic motion.

The above factors are included in all body movements in various degrees. The degree to which is used effectively in combination will determine the extent to which the movement is performed with skill. As mentioned previously, the area of movement education purports to give children freedom in exploring various forms of movement with reference to the above qualities.

In 1980 I conducted a national survey regarding trends in movement education and some interesting information was revealed. In approximately 45 percent of the cases the movement education "approach" was gaining in popularity whereas in 37 percent of the cases it was declining. In 18 percent of the cases interest in the approach appeared to be remaining the same. Interest in this approach appears to have begun in the mid-1960s, reaching a peak about 1970. In some parts of the country this interest has been maintained while in others it has waned. General reasons given for the gain in popularity include (1) it is an important part of a balanced program at the primary level, (2) it helps children become more aware of their bodies, and (3) there is an interest in all aspects of elementary school physical education. Reasons for a decline in popularity were (1) it overlooks the planned approach with instruction in various motor skill techniques, (2) traditional teachers will not subscribe to it, and (3) there is too much confusion about it as teachers do not understand the purpose of it.

In general, it appears that interest in the movement education approach has leveled off at least to a certain extent. In some cases physical educators divided into "camps" with respect to what some have referred to as the "traditional" approach as compared to the "movement education approach." This is most unfortunate because we should be working in the direction of what is in the best interest of children.

It is interesting to note that there is little research to support either approach unequivocally when used in the extreme. What little evidence is available suggests that a combination of the so-called traditional approach and the so-called movement education approach may be the most beneficial in teaching physical education activities to elementary school children.

Certainly any approach that is taken in our dealings with children as far as movement experiences are concerned should first and foremost take into account how well their needs are being met, along with procedures which are compatible with what we know about the learning process and how children learn.

It should appear evident from this short historical background that elementary school physical education has traveled a strange and sometimes hazardous road in reaching the level of importance that is attributed to it in modern education. However, in spite of the various pitfalls this area of education in the elementary school has forged ahead to the point where there has been almost unbelievable and unparalled progress in the past few years. This does not mean that the proponents for this area of education can become lethargic. Much needs to be done to continue to interpret the place and function of physical education in the modern elementary school curriculum, as well as to provide ways and means whereby physical education learning experiences can become even more valuable in the total growth and development of the elementary school child.

SOME CONCEPTS OF CHILD DEVELOPMENT AND THEIR MEANING FOR PHYSICAL EDUCATION

There has been a great deal of observation and research dealing with the growth and development of children. This information is most important to teachers in that it provides them with an understanding of how children might grow and develop in a way that is appropriate to their innate capacities and the environment in modern society.

Child development specialists have formulated what are termed concepts of physical, social, emotional, and intellectual development. A few examples of some of these are given here together with suggestions of their meaning for physical education. (It should be understood that only a partial list of these concepts is submitted and that the interested reader can resort to appropriate sources for a more detailed listing.)

CONCEPTS OF PHYSICAL DEVELOPMENT

Physical Development and Change Are Continuous

In the early years of the child's life, physical education programs might well be characterized by large muscle activities. As the child develops, more difficult types of skills and activities can be introduced so that physical education experiences progress in a way that is compatible with the child's development.

Physical Development Is Controlled by Both Heredity and Environment

The physical education program should be planned in a way to meet the innate capacities of each child. The teacher should attempt to establish an environmental climate where all children have an equal opportunity for wholesome participation.

Differences in Physical Development Occur at Each Age Level

This implies that there should be a wide variety of activities to meet the needs of children at the various developmental levels. While gearing activities to meet the needs of a particular group of children the teacher should also attempt to provide for individual differences of children within the group.

Sex Differences in Development Occur at Different Ages

At the early levels of the elementary school, perhaps in grades one and two, boys and girls can participate satisfactorily together in most activities. As sex differences involving such factors as strength and endurance occur, provision might well be made for the separation of boys and girls in certain types of activities.

Needs of a Physical Nature Must Be Satisfied if a Child Is to Function Effectively

Physical education lessons should be planned to provide an adequate activity yield. At the same time the teacher should be aware of fatigue symptoms so that children are not likely to go beyond their physical capacity. Physical education programs should be vigorous enough to meet the physical needs of children and at the same time motivating enough so that they will desire to perpetuate the physical education experiences outside of the school.

CONCEPTS OF SOCIAL DEVELOPMENT

Man Is a Social Being

Opportunities should be provided for children to experience follower-ship as well as leadership. The teacher should capitalize upon the social skills that are inherent in most physical education activities.

Interpersonal Relationships Have Social Needs as Their Basis

All children should be given an equal opportunity in physical education participation. Moreover, the teacher should impress upon children their importance to the group. This can be done in connection with the team or group effort that is essential to successful participation.

A Child Can Develop His Self-Concept Through Undertaking Roles

A child is more likely to be aware of his particular abilities if he is given the opportunity to play the different positions in a team game. Rotation of such responsibilities as squad or group leaders tends to provide opportunity for self-expression of children through role playing.

There Are Various Degrees of Interaction Between Individuals and Groups

Physical education provides a potentially excellent setting for the child to develop interpersonal interaction. The teacher has an opportunity to observe the children in a movement situation rather than in only a sedentary situation; consequently, he or she is in a good position to guide integrative experiences by helping children see the importance of satisfactory interrelationships in physical education group situations.

Choosing and Being Chosen, an Expression of a Basic Need, Is a Foundation of Interpersonal Relationships

As far as possible children should be given the responsibility for choosing teammates, partners, and the like. However, great caution should be taken by the teacher to see that this is carried out in an equitable way. The teacher should devise ways of choice so that certain children are not always selected last or left out entirely.

CONCEPTS OF EMOTIONAL DEVELOPMENT

An Emotional Response May Be Brought About by a Goal's Being Furthered or Thwarted

The teacher should make a very serious effort to assure successful experience for every child in his physical education activities. This can be accomplished in part by attempting to provide for individual differences within given physical education activities. The physical education setting should be such that each child derives a feeling of personal worth through making some sort of positive contribution.

Self-Realization Experiences Should Be Constructive

The opportunity for creative experience inherent in many physical education activities affords the child an excellent chance for self-realization through physical expression. Teachers might well consider planning with children to see that activities are meeting their needs and as a result involve a constructive experience.

As the Child Develops, His Emotional Reactions Tend to Become Less Violent and More Discriminating

A well-planned program and progressive sequence of physical education activities can provide for release of aggression in a socially acceptable manner.

Depending on Certain Factors, a Child's Own Feelings May Be Accepted or Rejected by the Individual

The child's physical education experience should make him feel good and have confidence in himself. Satisfactory self-concept seems closely related to body control; therefore, physical education experiences might be considered as one of the best ways of contributing to it.

CONCEPTS OF INTELLECTUAL DEVELOPMENT

Children Differ in Intelligence

Teachers should be aware that poor performance of some children in physical education activities might be due to the fact that they have not understood directions. Differences in intelligence levels as well as in physical skill and ability need to be taken into account in the planning of physical education lessons.

Mental Development Is Rapid in Early Childhood and Slows Down Later

Children want and need challenging kinds of physical education experiences. Physical education lessons should be planned and taught much in the same way as other curriculum areas of the elementary school. This precludes a program that is devoted entirely to what has been called "nondirected play."

Intelligence Develops Through the Interaction of the Child and His Environment

Movement experiences in physical education involve a process of interacting with the environment. There are many problem-solving opportunities in the well-planned physical education environment and hence the child can be presented with challenging learning situations.

Situations Which Encourage Total Personality Development Appear to Provide the Best Situation for Intellectual Development

The potential for total personality development (physical, social, emotional, and intellectual) is more evident in physical education than in most of the other curriculum areas in the elementary school. If one were to analyze each of the curriculum areas for its potentialities for physical, social, emotional, and intellectual development, it is doubtful that any one of these areas would compare with the potential that is inherent in the physical education learning situation.

OBJECTIVES OF PHYSICAL EDUCATION

It should be readily discerned that the component elements of total development become the objectives of physical education in the elementary school. These elements have been expressed in terms of physical, social, emotional, and intellectual development of children of elementary school age, and as such become the physical, social, emotional, and intellectual objectives of elementary school physical education.

The Physical Objective

This objective should imply the development of skill and ability in a variety of physical education activities together with organic development commensurate with vigor, vitality, balance, flexibility, and neuro-muscular coordination.

The Social Objective

This objective should imply satisfactory experiences in how to meet and get along with others, development of proper attitudes toward one's peers, and the development of a sense of values.

The Emotional Objective

This objective should imply that sympathetic guidance should be provided in meeting anxieties, joys, sorrows, and help given in developing aspirations, affections, and security.

The Intellectual Objective

This objective should imply the development of specific knowledge pertaining to rules, regulations, and strategies involved in a variety of worthwhile physical education learning experiences. In addition, this objective should be concerned with the value of physical education as a most worthwhile learning medium in the development of concepts and understanding in other curriculum areas—cognitive motor learning— the major concern of Part III of this book.

CONSIDERATIONS IN PLANNING PHYSICAL EDUCATION EXPERIENCES

Every school experience should contribute to the growth and development of children. If physical education is to play its part in meeting the goals of education, it must be carefully planned to meet the developmental needs of children at each grade level.

If you remember the objectives of physical education just discussed you are ready to take the first step in planning for desirable and worthwhile physical education experiences for children. That is, you are able to state clearly what you hope to accomplish in physical education. The second step is to determine what physical education experiences should be provided so that the objectives can be reached.

However, there is a third essential consideration to take into account. Although the ultimate objectives are the same for all grade levels the *means* used to achieve these objectives are different in certain ways. This is to say that the physical education experiences provided in the primary grades should differ from those offered in the intermediate grades. The children in grades kindergarten through grade three are different developmentally speaking, from those in grades four through six. Children in each stage of the developmental process have their unique characteristics. An important aspect of program planning is that which is concerned with the selection of physical education activities that are compatible with the developmental level of the children to be taught. The important thing is to understand the basic concept of adjusting physical education experiences to meet the changing needs, interests, and abilities of children as they grow and develop.

Let us use mathematics to illustrate how another curriculum area is adjusted to the mental development of children as they progress through the grades. Simple number concepts are developed in the primary grades such as counting and understanding numbers and numeration systems. The progression for learning the various operations in arithmetic begins with addition, the least difficult, and proceeds through the more difficult operations of subtraction, multiplication, and division.

Virtually everyone accepts this progression of skills from the least difficult in mathematics, reading, the development of science concept and the like. Far fewer people realize that the need for such progression is just as great in physical education. On average, the primary school child is simply not ready for highly complex games like football. It is, of course, true that we occasionally find some children who have unusual talent in some sport. There are also child geniuses in mathematics, music, and art, but no one claims that elementary school offerings for *all* children should be adjusted to the very small number of children who are exceptional in ability.

Qualified physical educators recognize that if activities are misplaced in the physical education curriculum, they may lose their value and may even detract from rather than contribute to optimum growth and development of children. For this reason great care must be exercised in the proper selection of physical education curriculum content.

ELEMENTARY SCHOOL PHYSICAL
EDUCATION CURRICULUM CONTENT

As mentioned previously, generally speaking, there are three broad categories of physical education activities which help to meet certain recognized needs of elementary school children. These categories involve (1) active games, (2) rhythmic activities, and (3) self-testing activities. Although these categories remain much the same for all the grade levels, the complexity of activities within each category increases. There is still another category which is involved in all of the above and this is the area of *basic movement and fundamental skills*. Being able to move effectively and efficiently is directly related to the proficiency with which the child will be able to perform the various fundamental motor skills. In turn, the success children will have in physical education activities will be dependent upon their proficiency of performance of these skills. This is the subject of the following chapter.

Chapter 2

LEARNING OF MOTOR SKILLS

As mentioned previously, curricular motor learning is involved with the learning of motor skills. Thus, this chapter will go into detail with regard to motor skill learning.

Just as the perception of symbols is concerned with reading readiness, so is basic movement an important factor in readiness to perform in various kinds of physical education activities. Since proficient performance of physical education activities is dependent upon skill of body movement, the ability of the child to move effectively should be readily discerned. This could be an important function of the area previously described as movement education. Some authorities in movement education subscribe to this notion by maintaining that sometimes at a very early age a child may discover and use combinations of movements which in reality are—or will eventuate into—specialized motor skills normally used in the complex organization of a game or dance.

In this sense, the child is becoming ready for direct skill teaching and learning. With proper teacher guidance the basic movements that he has developed on his own can be improved in terms of proper principles of body mechanics and commensurate with his natural ability. The important factor is that in the early stages the child has been made to feel comfortable with the way he moves and thus is in a better position to learn correct performance of skills.

Skills are the scientific way to move the body and/or its segments in such a way as to expend a minimum amount of energy requirement, but achieve maximum results. Performance of specific skills has been arrived at by scientific insight from such fields as anatomy and kinesiology, which suggests to us how the body can move to achieve maximum efficiency.

Other things being equal, the degree of proficient performance of a skill by any individual is directly related to his or her innate capacity; that is, each individual is endowed with a certain amount of native ability. Through such factors as good teaching, motivation, and the like, attempts are made to help the child perform to the best of his or her particular ability and attain the highest *skill level.*

FACTORS INVOLVED IN
SKILL TEACHING AND LEARNING

Because of the importance of the development of certain kinds of motor skills for best performance in physical education activities, one would think that this area of teaching in physical education would receive a great amount of attention. On the contrary, the teaching of physical education motor skills has been one of the most neglected phases of the entire elementary school physical education program. It is indeed a paradoxical situation because the successful performance and resultant enjoyment received from a physical education activity depends in a large measure upon how well the child can perform the skill elements involved. Yet, at a time in the child's life that is ideal for learning motor skills, we find that in far too many instances this important phase is left almost entirely to chance.

Although each child is born with a certain potential capacity, teachers should not subscribe to the notion that skills are a part of the child's inheritance. Skills must be learned. In order that a child can participate satisfactorily with his peers, he or she must be given the opportunity to learn the skills under the careful guidance of competent teachers.

The elementary school has long been considered the educational segment of an individual's life that provides the best opportunity for a solid educational foundation. The need for the development of basic skills in reading, writing, and arithmetic has seldom, if ever, been challenged as an essential purpose of the elementary school. Why, then should there be a neglect of such an important aspect of learning as that existing in the development of motor skills?

Perhaps the ideal time to learn motor skills is in childhood. The muscular pliability of the young child is such that there is a desirable setting for the acquisition of various kinds of motor skills. The child is at a stage in life when there is a great deal of time for practice—a most important factor because children need practice in order to learn—and at this age level they do not seem to become weary of repeating the same thing over and over again. In addition, the young child has a limited number of established skills to obstruct the learning of new skills. Skill learning, therefore, should be facilitated provided competent teaching in the area of physical education motor skills is available.

Experimental research on the influence of specific instruction on various kinds of motor skills is somewhat limited. More and more scientific evidence is being accumulated, however, which appears to indicate that children in the early elementary school years are mature enough to benefit by instruction in skills such as throwing and jumping. Unfortunately, this type of instruction is lacking in far too many elementary school physical education programs.

Following are some suggested guidelines that teachers might take into account in the teaching of skills.

1. The teacher should become familiar with the skills involved in the various physical education activities. This means that it will be necessary for the teacher to analyze each activity to determine the extent of the skill requirements.

2. In considering the teaching of physical education skills, the teacher should recognize that skills include the following three components: (a) preparing for the movement, (b) executing the movement, and (c) following through. For example, in throwing a ball the individual prepares for the movement by assuming the proper position to throw; he completes the actual throwing of the ball; and finally there is a follow-through action of the arm after the ball leaves the hand. All of these elements are essential to satisfactory performance of this particular skill.

3. The skill should be taught correctly from the beginning; otherwise children may have to do a considerable amount of "unlearning" at a later stage of development.

4. When an error in skill performance is observed, it should be corrected immediately. This can be done under the guidance of the teacher by evaluating the child's performance with him. Correction of errors in skill performance is essential, first because continued repetition may formulate the faulty practice into a habit, and second because the child will have less difficulty learning more complex skills if he has previously learned easier skills correctly. Teacher should recognize that while there are general patterns for the best performance of skills, individual differences must be considered. This implies that a child should be permitted to devi-

ate from a standard if he is able to perform a skill satisfactorily in a manner peculiar to his individual abilities.

5. The greatest amount of time should be spent on skill learning that involves immediate application. In other words, the child should have use for the physical education skills being taught so that he can properly apply them commensurate with his stage of development.

6. There is some indication that rhythmic accompaniment is important in the learning of skills. Although the evidence is not definitive and clear-cut, various studies tend to support this contention.

LOCOMOTOR SKILLS

Locomotor skills involve changes in body position that propel the body over the surface area with the impetus being given by the feet and legs. There are five basic types of these skills: namely, walking, running, leaping, jumping, hopping, and three combination skills, which are galloping, skipping, and sliding. The first five of these are performed with an even rhythm, and the last three are done with an uneven rhythm. Locomotor skills require a certain amount of strength and the development of the important sensory-motor mechanisms that are concerned with balance. They also require various degrees of neuromotor coordination for proficient performance.

All of the locomotor skills should be learned by the elementary school-age child. One reason is that these skills comprise the basic requirements for proficiency of performance in the activities contained in a well-planned physical education program for children. Also, it is important that the child be helped early in life to gain control over the physical aspect of personality, or what is known as *basic body control.*

Teachers should have certain basic knowledge about the locomotor skills so that they will be alert to improve performance of these skills. The following generalized information is intended for this purpose.

Walking

Walking is the child's first experience with bipedal locomotion. He starts to propel himself over the surface area with uneven, full-sole steps (flat-footedness). He is generally referred to as a "toddler," a term that is perhaps derived from the word "tottering." He appears to be tottering to keep in an upright position, which is indicative of the problems he is having with balance and the force of gravity. At about four years of age, on the average, the child's pattern of walking approximates that of an adult.

Ordinarily, when the child is learning to walk, his only teachers are his family members. Because of this, he is not likely to benefit from instruction on correct procedure. As a result, the very important aspect of foot position is overlooked. Possibly because of this, many children enter school walking in the "toeing out" position rather than pointing the toes straight ahead. Poor walking habits, if allowed to persist, can place undue amounts of strain on certain body parts that in turn may contribute to lack of proficiency in body movement.

Walking involves transferring the weight from one foot to the other. The walk is started with a push-off backward against the surface area with the ball and toes of the foot. After this initial movement the leg swings forward from the hip, the heel of the other foot is placed down, the outer half of the foot next, and the next push-off is made with the toes pointing straight ahead. Walking is used in such physical education activities as walking to rhythmical accompaniment, combining the walk with other movements in various dance activities, walking about in movement songs, and walking around a circle preparatory to the start of a circle game activity.

Running

At about 18 months of age, the average child develops a movement that appears to be in between a walk and a run. This is to say that the walking pattern is accelerated, but does not approximate running form. Usually, it is not before ages five or six that the child's running form becomes similar to that used by an adult. As the child gets older he is able to increase his speed of running as well as be able to run greater distances.

Like walking, running involves transferring the weight from one foot to the other, but the rate of speed is increased. The ball of the foot touches the surface area first, and the toes point straight ahead. The body is momentarily suspended in the air when there is no contact with the surface area. This differs from the walk in which contact with either foot is always maintained with the surface area. In the run, there is more flexion at the knee, which involves a higher leg lift. There is also a higher arm lift, with flexion at the elbow reaching a point of about a right angle. In running, there is more of a forward lean than in walking, and in both cases the head points straight ahead. In many instances, the child who has not been taught to run correctly will violate certain mechanical principles by having a backward rather than forward lean, by carrying the arms too high, and by turning the head to the side rather than looking straight ahead.

Running is probably the most used of all the locomotor skills in physical education, particularly with most game activities.

Leaping

Leaping, like walking and running, is performed with an even rhythm like a slow run, with one essential difference: the push-off is up and then forward, with the feeling of suspension "up and over." The landing should be on the ball of the foot with sufficient flexion at the knee to absorb the shock.

Although leaping is not used frequently as a specific locomotor skill in many physical education activities, there are certain reasons why it is important that children become proficient in this skill. For example, the leap can be combined with the run to leap over an object so as not to deviate from the running pattern. In addition, in retrieving a ball that has been thrown or hit high, a leap for the ball can help the child to catch it "on the run" and thus continue with the running pattern, rather than having to stop his movement.

Specific uses of leaping consist of its performance by children in creative rhythms, where they move as the music makes them feel like moving, or in the case of a game like *Leap the Brook*, the object is to leap over an area while gradually increasing the distance.

Jumping

In a sense, jumping is somewhat like walking and running in that the movement pattern is similar. However, jumping requires elevation of the body off the surface area, and thus more strength is needed to apply force for this purpose. Usually, the child's first experience with a movement approximating jumping occurs when he steps from a higher to a lower level, as in the case of going downstairs. Although there are many variations in the jumping performance of children, generally speaking, they tend to improve their performance as they get older, with improvement tending to be more pronounced for boys than girls.

Jumping is accomplished by pushing off with both feet and landing on both feet or pushing off with one foot and landing on both feet. Since absorption of shock is important in jumping, the landing should be with flexed knees and on the balls of the feet.

Games such as basketball and volleyball require skill in jumping in order to gain success in such activities. The jump becomes a complete activity in itself when children compete against their own performance in individual jumping. This can be done with the standing broad jump (taking off and landing on both feet) or the long jump (running to a point and taking off on one foot and landing on both feet).

Hopping

While hopping is the least difficult of the even rhythmic locomotor skills to describe, at the same time it is perhaps the most difficult to execute. Hopping involves taking off and landing on the same foot. Thus, hopping is a more complex aspect of the jump because the body is elevated from the surface area by the action of only one foot. Not only is greater strength needed for the hop, but also a more refined adjustment of balance is required because of the smaller base of support.

Hopping, as such, is not used frequently as a specific skill in many physical education activities. Exceptions include such dance steps as the *schottische*, which involves a pattern of "step-step-step-hop-step-hop-step-hop," or the hopping relay in which children hop to a point on one foot and return on the other foot. In addition, it should be obvious that such games as *hopscotch* require skill in the ability to hop.

Even though hopping is not a specific skill used in most physical education activities, one of the more important reasons why children should become proficient in this locomotor skill is that it can help them regain balance in any kind of activity where they have temporarily "lost their footing." When this occurs, the child can use the hop to keep his balance and remain in an upright position while getting the temporarily incapacitated foot into action.

Galloping

The skill of galloping is a combination of the basic pattern of walk and leaping and is performed with an uneven rhythm. Since an uneven rhythmic movement requires more neuromotor coordination, the ability to gallop is developed later than those locomotor movements requiring an even rhythm. The child is likely to learn to gallop before he learns to skip, and about one-half of the children are able to perform at least an approximation of a galloping movement by about the age of four. Between the ages of six and seven most children can perform this movement.

Galloping can be explained by pretending that one foot is injured. A step is taken with the lead foot, but the "injured" foot can bear very little weight and is brought up only behind the other one and not beyond it. A transfer of weight is made to the lead foot, and thus a fast limp is really a gallop.

Galloping is a skill that does not have prevalent use as a specific skill in most physical education activities. One very important exception is its use as a fundamental rhythm when the children become "galloping horses" to appropriate rhythmical accompaniment. One of the most important factors about learning to gallop is that it helps children to be able to change direction in a forward and backward plane more easily. Backward galloping can be done by starting with the lead foot to the back. If a child is proficient in galloping, he will likely be more successful in game activities that require a forward and/or backward movement for successful performance in that particular activity.

Skipping

Although skipping requires more coordination than galloping, some children will perform variations of the skip around four years of age. With proper instruction, a majority of children should be able to accomplish this movement by age six.

Skipping can be taught from the walk. A strong push-off should be emphasized. The push-off should be such a forceful upward one that the foot leaves the surface area. In order to maintain balance a hop is taken. The sequence is step, push-off high, hop. The hop occurs on the same foot that was pushing off, and this is the skip. The two actions cause it to be uneven as to rhythm, with a strong or long action (step) and a short one (hop).

The skill of skipping is rarely used as a specific locomotor skill in many physical education activities. It does find limited use, however, as a fundamental rhythm when children skip to a musical accompaniment, when used in certain movement songs and dances, and when skipping around a circle preparatory to the start of certain circle games.

Sliding

Sliding is much the same as the gallop, but movement is in a sideward direction. One foot is drawn up to the lead foot; weight is shifted from the lead foot to the drawing foot and back again. As in the case with other locomotor skills that are uneven in rhythm, sliding is not used frequently as a specific skill in most physical education activities. The one main exception is its use in many of the social or ballroom dance patterns.

The important feature of gaining proficiency in the skill of sliding is that it helps the child to be able to change direction skillfully in a lateral plane. Many games involving guarding an opponent, such as basketball, require skill in sliding for success in the game. When a child has developed the skill of sliding from side to side, he does not have to cross his feet and thus can change direction laterally much more easily.

AXIAL SKILLS

Axial skills are nonlocomotor in nature. They can be performed with some parts of the body remaining in contact with the surface area or the body as a whole in gross movement. Included among the axial skills are swinging, bending, stretching, pulling, pushing, and the rotation movements of turning and twisting.

Each of these movements are required at one time or another in the performance of practically all physical education activities. Proficiency of performance of the axial skills will improve performance in locomotor skills; for example, the importance of arm swinging in running. When children can perform the axial skills with grace and facility there is a minimum expenditure of energy, and better performance results.

AUXILIARY SKILLS

There are certain skills that are not ordinarily classified as either locomotor or axial. However, they are most important in the successful performance of most physical education activities. These skills are arbitrarily identified here as auxiliary skills. Among some of the more important of this type of skill are: starting, stopping, dodging, pivoting, falling, and landing.

Starting

In games that require responding to a stimulus, such as running to a goal on the word "go," a quick start is an important contribution to success. How well a child will be able to "start" depends upon his reaction time and speed of movement. Reaction time is the amount of time that it takes from the time a signal is given until the onset of the initial movement. Speed of movement is concerned with how fast the person completes the initial movement. Although the factors concerned with starting are innate, they improve with practice. When a teacher observes children as being "slow starters," additional help should be given to improve this skill.

Stopping

The skill of stopping is very important because all locomotor movements culminate with this skill. Numerous game activities require quick stopping for successful performance.

Two ways of stopping are the *stride* stop and the *skip* stop. The stride stop involves stopping in running stride. There is flexion at the knees and a slight backward lean to maintain balance. This method of stopping can be used when the performer is moving at a slow speed. The skip stop should be used when there is fast movement, and the performer needs to come to a quick stop. This is accomplished with a hop on either foot, with the other foot making contact with the surface area almost simultaneously. Because of the latter movement, this method of stopping is sometimes called the *jump* stop, because it appears that the performer is landing on both feet at the same time.

Starting and stopping can be practiced in an activity situation with the game *Start and Stop*. In this game, the children are in a straight line with the teacher at the goal line some distance away. The teacher calls "Start," and on this signal all the children run forward. The teacher then calls "Stop," and anyone moving after the signal must return to the starting line. This procedure is continued until one or more children have reached the goal line. The teacher should be alert to detect starting and stopping form.

Dodging

Dodging involves changing direction while running. The knees are bent, and the weight is transferred in the dodging direction. This movement is sometimes referred to as "veering" or "weaving." After a dodge is made, the performer can continue in the different direction with a push-off from the surface area with the foot to which the weight was previously transferred.

The importance of skill in dodging is seen in game activities where getting away from an opponent (tag games) or an object (dodge ball) is necessary.

Pivoting

Whereas dodging is used to change direction during body movement, pivoting is employed to change direction while the body is stationary. One foot is kept in contact with the surface area, while the other foot is used to push off. A turn is made in the desired direction with the weight on the foot that has maintained contact with the surface area. The angle of the pivot (turn) is determined by the need in the particular situation. This angle is not likely to be over 180 degrees, as might be the case in pivoting away from an opponent in basketball.

Theoretically, the pivot is executed on only one foot; however, a *reverse turn* is sometimes referred to as a "two-foot" pivot. In this case, a complete turn to the opposite direction is made with both feet on the surface area. With one foot ahead of the other, the heels are raised, and a turn is made with weight equally distributed on both feet.

Pivoting is important in the performance of many kinds of physical education activities, such as various forms of dance and game activities, where quick movements are necessary while the body remains stationary. This is particularly true in games like basketball and speedball where a limited number of steps can be taken while in possession of the ball.

Landing

Landing is concerned with the body coming to the surface area from a height or distance. Absorption when landing is accomplished by bending the knees. The weight is on the balls of the feet, and there is flexion at the ankle and knee joints. After landing, the performer comes to an upright position with the arms in a sideward position so as to keep the body in balance.

Many game activities such as basketball, volleyball, and touch football require the performer to leave the surface area, which makes the skill of landing important. In addition, vaulting over objects in apparatus activities requires skill in landing, not only for good performance, but for safety as well.

Falling

In those activities that require staying in an upright position, emphasis, of course, should be on maintaining this position. Nevertheless, there are occasions when a performer loses balance and falls to the surface area. Whenever possible, a fall should be taken in such a way that injury is least likely to occur. One way to accomplish this is to attempt to "break the fall" with the hands. Relaxation and flexion at the joints that put the performer in a "bunched" position are helpful in avoiding injury when falling to the surface area. Practice of the correct way to make contact with the surface area when falling can take place in connection with the various rolls in tumbling activities.

SKILLS OF PROPULSION AND RETRIEVAL

Skills which involve propelling and retrieving objects, in most cases a ball, are used in many types of game activities. It will be the purpose of this section of the chapter to provide the reader with knowledge of which is important to an understanding of such propelling and retrieving skills as throwing, striking, kicking, and catching.

Throwing

The skill of throwing involves the release of a ball with one or both hands. In general, there are three factors concerned with success in throwing. These are the accuracy or direction of the throw, the distance in which a ball must be thrown, and the amount of force needed to propel the ball.

Any release of an object from the hand or hands could be considered as an act of throwing. Thought of in these terms, the average infant of six months is able to perform a reasonable facsimile of throwing from a sitting position. It has been estimated that by four years of age, about 20 percent of the children show at least a degree of proficiency in throwing. This ability tends to increase rapidly, and between the ages of five or six, over three-fourths of the children can attain a reasonable degree of proficiency as previously defined here.

Gender differences in the early throwing behavior of children tend to favor boys. At all age levels, boys are generally superior to girls in throwing for distance. There is not such a pronounced gender difference in throwing for accuracy, although the performance of boys in this aspect tends to exceed that of girls.

There are generally three accepted throwing patterns. These are the (1) underarm pattern, (2) sidearm pattern, and (3) overarm pattern. It should be noticed that although the ball is released by one or both hands, the term "arm" is used in connection with the various patterns. The reason is that the patterns involve a "swing" of the arm.

Underarm Throwing Pattern

The child ordinarily begins the underarm throwing pattern by releasing the ball from both hands. However, he is soon able to release with one hand, especially when the ball is small enough to grip.

At the starting position, the thrower stands facing in the direction of the throw. The feet should be in a parallel position and slightly apart. The right arm is in a position nearly perpendicular to the surface area. (All of the descriptions involving the skills of propulsion and retrieval are for the right-handed child. In the case of the left-handed child, just the opposite should apply.) To start the throw, the right arm is brought back (back swing) to a position where it is about parallel with the surface area. Simultaneously, there is a slight rotation of the body to the right with most of the weight transferred to the right foot. As the arm comes forward (front swing) a step is taken with the left foot. (Stepping out with the opposite foot of the swinging arm is known as the *principle of opposition.*) The ball is released on the front swing when the arm is about parallel to the surface area. During the process of the arm swing, the arm is straight, prescribing a semicircle with no flexion at the elbow. The right foot is carried forward as a part of the follow-through after the release.

The underarm throwing pattern is used in games that involve passing the ball from one person to another over a short distance. It is also used for pitching in the game of softball and other baseball-type games.

Sidearm Throwing Pattern

Aside from the direction the thrower faces and the plane of the arm swing, the mechanical principles applied in the sidearm throwing pattern are essentially the same as the underarm throwing pattern.

The thrower faces at a right angle to the direction of the throw, whereas in the underarm throwing pattern he faces in the direction of the throw. The arm is brought to the backswing in a horizontal plane or a position parallel to the surface area. Body rotation and weight shift is the same as in the underarm pattern. The arm remains straight and a semicircle is prescribed from the backswing to the release of the ball on the front swing.

The side arm throwing pattern will ordinarily be used to propel a ball that is too large to grip with one hand. Thus, on the backswing the opposite hand helps to control the ball until there is sufficient momentum during the swing. Greater distance can be obtained with the sidearm throwing pattern with a ball too large to grip, but accuracy is more difficult to achieve.

Overarm Throwing Pattern

Again the basic body mechanics of the overarm throwing pattern are essentially the same as the two previous patterns. The thrower faces in the same direction as for the sidearm throwing pattern, i.e., at a right angle to the direction of the throw. Depending upon individual differences, this position may vary. An essential difference in the overarm throwing pattern is the position of the arm. Whereas, in the two previous patterns the arm was kept straight, in the overarm throwing pattern there is flexion at the elbow. Thus, on the backswing the arm is brought back with the elbow bent and with the arm at a right angle away from the body. The arm is then brought forward and the ball is released in a "whiplike" motion at about the height of the shoulder. Foot and arm follow through is the same as with the underarm and sidearm throwing patterns. This pattern is used for throwing a ball that can be gripped with the fingers in such games as softball where distance as well as accuracy are important.

Striking

Striking involves propelling a ball with a part of the body, ordinarily the hand, as in handball or with an implement such as a bat in softball. The object to be struck can be stationary, e.g., batting a ball from a batting tee or moving, e.g., batting a pitched ball in softball.

Some motor development specialists have identified a reasonable facsimile of striking in infancy associated with angry children throwing "nothing" at each other or an adult.

It has long been known that as early as the age of three, verbal direction to children will educe a sidearm striking pattern with a plastic paddle when a tennis ball is suspended in a stationary position at about waist high. In addition, it has been found that at age three, the child will have a degree of success with the sidearm throwing pattern in striking a light ball when tossed slowly to him.[1]

The principles of body mechanics and the striking patterns are essentially the same as the three previously mentioned throwing patterns—underarm, sidearm, and overarm. The same movements are applied, but in order to propel an object by striking, greater speed is needed with the striking movement. For example, greater speed of movement is needed in the underarm striking pattern when serving a volleyball, than in releasing a ball with a short toss in the underarm throw.

Kicking

Kicking involves propelling a ball with either foot. As early as age two the average child is able to maintain his balance on one foot and propel a stationary ball with the other foot. At this early age the child is likely to have limited action of the kicking foot with little or no follow through. With advancing age, better balance and strength are maintained that by age six, the child can develop a full leg backswing and a body lean into the kick of a stationary ball.

In kicking, contact with the ball is made with the (1) inside of the foot,

---

[1]Halverson, L. E. and Roberton, M. A., Motor pattern development in young children, *Research Abstracts*, Washington, DC, American Association for Health, Physical Education, and Recreation, 1966.

(2) outside of the foot, or (3) with the instep of the foot. With the exception of these positions of the foot the mechanical principles of kicking are essentially the same. The kicking leg is swung back with flexion at the knee. The leg swings forward with the foot making contact with the ball. As in the case of the skill of striking, contact with the ball in kicking can be made when the ball is either stationary or moving.

There is not complete agreement though, in terms of progress in which the skill of kicking is learned. On the basis of personal experience and discussion with successful teachers, I recommend the following sequence.

Stationary

The ball and the kicker remain stationary, and the kicker stands beside the ball and kicks it. The kicker is concerned only with the leg movement, and it is more likely that the head will be kept down with the eyes on the ball at the point of contact.

Stationary and Run

This means that the ball is in a stationary position and that the kicker takes a short run up to the ball before kicking it. This is more difficult, as the kicker must time and coordinate the run to make proper contact with the ball.

Kick from Hands

This is referred to as "punting," as in football and soccer. The ball is dropped from the hands of the kicker, and he takes one or two steps and kicks the ball as it drops. He is kicking a moving ball, but he has control over the movement of the ball before kicking it.

Kicking from a Pitcher

This means that another person pitches or rolls the ball to the kicker as in the game of *kickball.* This is perhaps the most difficult kick because the kicker must kick a moving ball that is under the control of another person.

Catching

Catching with the hands is the most frequently used retrieving skill. One of the child's first experiences with catching occurs at an early stage in life, as when he sits with his legs in a spread position and another person rolls a ball to him. By four years of age, about one-third of the children can retrieve a ball in aerial flight thrown from a short distance. Slightly over half of them can perform this feat by age five, and about two-thirds of them can accomplish this by age six.

There are certain basic mechanical principles that should be taken into account in the skill of catching. It is of importance that the catcher position himself as nearly "in line" with the ball as possible. In this position he will be better able to receive the ball near the center of gravity of the body. Another important factor is hand position. A ball will approach the catcher (1) at the waist, (2) above the waist, or (3) below the waist. When the ball approaches at about waist level, the palms should be facing each other with fingers pointing straight ahead. The "heels" of the hands should be close together depending upon the size of the ball, i.e., closer together for a small ball and farther apart for a large ball. When the ball approaches above the waist, the palms still face the ball but the fingers point downward, with the little fingers as close together as seems necessary, depending again upon the size of the ball. When the ball reaches the hands, it is brought in toward the body, i.e., the catcher "gives" with the catch in order to control the ball and absorb the shock. The position of the feet will likely depend upon the speed with which the ball approaches. Ordinarily, one foot should be in advance of the other in a stride position, with the distance determined by the speed of the approaching ball.

The next, and concluding, chapter in Part I describes the broad categories of physical education content in which these skills can be applied.

Chapter 3

CURRICULUM CONTENT IN WHICH MOTOR SKILLS ARE APPLIED

I n Chapter 1 I identified three broad categories of physical education curriculum content: (1) active games, (2) rhythmic activities, and (3) self-testing activities.

ACTIVE GAMES

For purposes of discussion here I will consider games as *active interactions of children in competitive and/or cooperative situations.* This description of games places emphasis on "active" games as opposed those that are "passive" in nature. This is to say that games in physical education are concerned with a total or near total physical response of children as they interact with each other.

Games not only play a very important part in the school program, but in society in general. The unique quality of games and their application to situations in everyday living have become a part of various colloquial expressions. In many instances, descriptive word phrases from games have become a part of daily vocabulary and appear frequently in news articles and other written material. These words and phrases are used to describe a situation that is so familiar in a game situation that they give a clear meaning to an event from real life.

Many of us have used, at one time or another, the expression "That's the way the ball bounces" to refer to a situation in which the outcome was not as desirable as was anticipated, or, "That's par for the course," meaning that the difficulty was anticipated, and the results were no better or no worse than expected. When we are "home free" we tend to refer to having gotten out of a tight situation, with results better than expected. The expression "The bases are loaded" describes a situation in which a critical point has been reached and there is much at stake on the next event or series of events. If you have "two strikes against you," you are operating at a grave disadvantage, and if someone "strikes out," he has failed.

It is interesting to consider how the game preferences of a particular country give insight into its culture, and this has been an important area of study and research by sociologists for many years. The national games, the popular games, and the historical games the people of nations engage in provide insight into their culture. They are as much a cultural expression as their books, theater, and art.

The physiological value of games has often been extolled because of the vigorous physical nature of many game activities in which children participate. Also, a great deal of credence has put in the potentialities for modifying human behavior within a social frame of reference, which many games tend to provide. For instance, it has been suggested that the game is probably the child's first social relationship with strangers and his first testing of self against others.

In general, games played in small groups are enjoyed by most children at the primary level. These games ordinarily involve a few simple rules and in some cases elementary strategy. Games that involve chasing and fleeing, tag, and one small group against another, as well as those involving fundamental skills, are best suited to children at the lower elementary levels. In addition, children at this age level enjoy the game with an element of surprise, such as those that involve running for a goal on a given signal.

Children at the intermediate level retain an interest in some of the games they played at the primary level, and some of them can be extended and made more difficult to meet the needs and interests of these older children. In addition, games may now be introduced that call for greater bodily control, finer coordination of hands, eyes, and feet, more strength, and the utilization of some of the basic skills acquired in previous grades.

It has been found that children in the intermediate grades and some as low as third grade can engage satisfactorily in various types of team games such as basketball, soccer, softball, flag football, and volleyball. These games as played at the high school or college level are ordinarily too highly organized and complex for the majority of intermediate level children. It is therefore necessary to modify these activities to meet the needs and interests of this age level. By way of illustration let us consider the game of basketball as played at the high school or college level. Players at these levels use the regulation size basketball of 29½ inches in circumference and the goal is at a height of 10 feet. For children at the intermediate level the game could be modified by using a smaller ball and lowering the goal. At this level more simple strategies also would be used in playing the game. Teachers should use their own ingenuity along with the help of children in modifying the highly organized games to adjust them for suitability for specific groups of intermediate level children.

One approach to the introduction of the more highly organized teams games is the use of *preparatory* games. These contain many of the same skills used in the advanced games. These are within the capacity of children at this age level and provide them with an opportunity to learn many of the basic skills and some of the rules of the more advanced games.

Classification of Games

Within the broad category of active games there are various ways in which these activities might be classified. Ordinarily, game classifications center around certain constant elements which are inherent in the games in a given classification. Among others, some of these elements include organization, formation, materials, function, place, and type. It should be borne in mind that precise classification is most difficult and that there is likely to be unavoidable overlapping from one classification to another.

Organization

In classifying games by organization it is a standard practice to consider two broad classifications—*low* organization and *high* organization. Games of low organization are those with a few simple rules and they do not require a high level of skill. On the contrary, games of high organization have definite and fixed rules. Highly organized games ordinarily require well-developed skills in their performance as well as the use of various kinds of tactics and strategy in playing the game.

Formation

Games classified by formation pertain to the kind of alignment necessary for playing the game. For example, among others there may be a circle formation, line formation, or file formation.

Materials

A broad classification of games in the use of materials would be those requiring the use of equipment and those not requiring it. A more specific classification in terms of materials would be ball games, net games, and the like.

Function

This classification refers to body function and more specifically to body skills such as running, throwing, and striking games.

Place

The two broad classifications as far as place is concerned are indoor and outdoor games. More specific classifications would take into account such kinds as playground games, gymnasium games, and classroom games.

Type

Examples of classification of games by type are the dodge ball type where the objective is to strike another with an object and for the opponent to dodge the object, and the baseball type played on a facsimile of a baseball diamond with a home base and one or more bases.

Progression in Games

Essentially, the progression in games is to get the activities in sequence and at the same time aligning it with the progression of difficulty of performance. This is to say that in the same manner as other learning sequences, for example, the arithmetic operations (addition-subtraction-multiplication-division), game activities should progress from the less difficult to the more complex.

There are a variety of different ways in which progression in game activities can be effected, and two such possibilities are considered here. These are: (1) progression of games of the same type, and (2) progression within the same game (modification).

Progression of Games of the Same Type

The games in which the basic objective is essentially the same and yet have so many variations may be considered as a specific type of game.

Dodgeball is a case in point. Since there are so many versions of dodgeball, these can be considered as games of the dodgeball type. The illustration of this aspect of progression shown here utilizes the games of *Roll Dodge, Circle Dodge,* and *Chain Dodge,* all of which are played in circle formation.

Since there are various ways of organizing dodgeball-type games, a comment about organization seems appropriate at this point. The kind of organization that I prefer involves dividing the large group into about four smaller groups. Each small group becomes the "dodgers" for a specific period of time while the other three groups are throwers. Each succeeding small group takes its place as dodgers. Each time a person in the group is hit with the ball, it counts a point against his group, and the group with the lowest score after all four groups have been dodgers is the winner. Organization of this type keeps all of the children in the game all of the time with no one being eliminated.

The game of Roll Dodge has a circle of throwers with a group of dodgers in the circle. Emphasis is placed only upon dodging. The throwers roll the ball back and forth across the surface area as rapidly as they can while the dodgers try to dodge the ball. Children should be encouraged to use the underarm throwing pattern and to release the ball quickly. The previously mentioned method of scoring can be used.

In Circle Dodge, the organization and scoring method is the same as for Roll Dodge. However, the emphasis is placed both upon dodging and attempting to strike the dodger. The ball is thrown rather than rolled, and the children can use either the underarm or sidearm throwing pattern.

In Chain Dodge, the dodgers make a chain by forming a file. Each player gets a firm hold around the waist of the player in front of him/her. (The players comprising the chain should be of the same gender because of the nature of the alignment). The only person eligible to be hit in the chain is the person at the end of the chain. Any type of throwing pattern can be used. (The throwers should be instructed to hit below the waist line so as to avoid injury). The throwers must move the ball rapidly to each other in various parts of the circle in order to make a hit, and the chain must move in such a way as to protect the person on the end of the chain. If the last person is hit, the game stops temporarily and he goes to the front of the chain, with the previous next-to-last player becoming the one on the end of the chain. The same scoring method prevails.

Progression Within the Same Game (Modification)

Modification of a game means that it is made more or less difficult to meet the needs of a particular group of children. In this case, the game will be made increasingly difficult and the game of *Call Ball* is used as an example.

The version of Call Ball used here would require six or more children comprising a circle. One child stands in the center of the circle holding a rubber ball. He tosses the ball into the air and at the same time calls out the name of one of the children. The child whose name is called attempts to catch the ball either on the first bounce or on the fly, depending upon the ability of the children. If the player whose name is called catches the ball, he changes places with the child in the center and the game continues in this manner. If the child whose name is called does not catch the ball, the thrower remains in the center of the circle and tosses the ball up again.

If desired, rather than having a child throw the ball into the air from the center of the circle, the game can be controlled by the teacher's assuming this position. The degree of difficulty in retrieving the ball can be decreased or increased by the number of times the ball bounces. For example, it is easier to retrieve the ball if it is allowed to bounce than if the child is required to catch it on the fly. In addition, if the teacher is the one to put the ball into play, the degree of difficulty in retrieval can be effected by how high or low the ball is thrown into the air. Another way to increase or decrease the difficulty is to make the circle of children larger or smaller as desired. The imaginative teacher could have several different combinations of these modifications and thus effect progression of the game within itself.

Competition and Cooperation in Games

It should be recalled that my description of active games took into account both cooperation and competitive situations. In view of the fact that there has been a considerable amount of interest in competitive activities for children of elementary school age, it seems appropriate that this be discussed as it relates to games.

It is interesting to note that the terms *cooperation* and *competition* are antonymous; therefore the reconciliation of children's competitive needs and cooperative needs is not an easy matter. In a sense, we are confronted with an ambivalent condition which if not carefully handled, could place children in a state of conflict. Horney recognized this well over half century ago when she indicated that on the one hand everything is done to spur us toward success, which means that we must not only be assertive but aggressive, able to push others out of the way. On the other hand, we are deeply imbued with ideals which declare that it is selfish to want anything for ourselves, that we should be humble, turn the other hand and be yielding.[1]

Thus, modern society not only rewards one kind of behavior (cooperation) but its direct opposite (competition). Perhaps more often than not our cultural demands sanction these rewards without provision of clear-cut standards of value with regard to specific conditions under which these forms of behavior might well be practiced. Therefore, the child is placed in somewhat of a quandary as to when to compete and when to cooperate.

More recently it has been found that competition does not necessarily lead to peak performance and may in fact interfere with achievement. In this connection Kohn[2] reported on a survey on the effect of competition on sports, business, and classroom achievement and found that 65 studies showed that cooperation promoted higher achievement than competition, eight showed the reverse and 36 showed no statistically significant difference. It was concluded that the trouble with competition is that it makes one person's success depend upon another's failure, and as a result when success depends on sharing resources, competition can get in the way.

In generalizing on the basis of the available evidence with regard to the subject of competition, it seems justifiable to formulate the following concepts.

1. Very young children in general are not very competitive but become more so as they grow older.
2. There is a wide variety in competition among children; that is, some are violently competitive, while others are mildly competitive, and still others are not competitive at all.
3. Boys tend to be more competitive than girls.
4. Competition should be adjusted so that there is not a preponderant number of winners over losers.

---

[1]Horney, Karen, *The Neurotic Personality of Our Times,* New York, W.W. Norton & Company, Inc., 1937.

[2]Kohn, A. *No Contest: The Case Against Competition* Boston, Houghton-Mifflin, 1986.

5. Competition and rivalry can sometimes produce results in effort and speed of accomplishment.

Teachers might well be guided by the above concepts. As far as active games are concerned they are not only a good medium for the various aspects of growth and development of children but, under the guidance of skillful teachers, they can also provide for competitive needs of children in a pleasurable and enjoyable way.

RHYTHMIC ACTIVITIES

Those human movement experiences that require some sort of rhythmical accompaniment may be placed in the broad category of rhythmic activities. As in the case of defining other terms throughout this text, the definition of rhythmic activities is arbitrary and is used for purposes of discussion here. I am aware that some authorities consider the meaning of the term *dance* to be a broader one than the term *rhythmic activities*. However, the point of view is that there are certain human movement experiences that require some form of rhythmical accompaniment that do not necessarily have the same objectives as those ordinarily associated with dance.

The term *rhythm* is derived from the Greek word *rhythmos*, which means "measured motion." One of the most desirable media for child expression through movement is found in rhythmic activities. One need look only to the functions of the human body to see the importance of rhythm in the life of young children. The heart beats in rhythm, the digestive processes function in rhythm, breathing is done in rhythm; in fact, almost anything in which human beings are involved in is done in a rhythmical pattern.

Status of Rhythmic Activities in Childhood Education

It is difficult to identify a precise time when rhythmic activities were introduced into the elementary schools of America. Perhaps one of the earliest attempts in this direction came around the turn of the century when John Dewey was director of the University of Chicago Laboratory School. At this time, Dewey had introduced folk dancing into the program, which could possibly be the first time such an activity took place in schools on such a formalized manner. Up until that time, rhythmic activities, if used at all, undoubtedly took place on a sporadic and spasmodic basis. For example, there were instances when certain types of singing games (now called movement songs) were a part of the "opening exercises" of some elementary schools.

During the decade preceding World War I, some aspects of nationality dances found their way into the school program. This ordinarily occurred in those large cities where certain ethnic backgrounds were predominant in a given neighborhood.

The period between the two world wars saw rhythmic activities introduced into more schools, and this was probably due to the fact that more emphasis was beginning to be placed on the social aspect of physical education. By the late 1920s, some elementary schools were allotting as much as 25 percent of the physical education time to rhythmic activities.

In these modern times, rhythmic activities are characterized by diversity. This aspect of physical education encompasses a wide variety of activities, and there appears to be little standardization from one school to another. Perhaps one of the reasons for this is the variation in teacher preparation and the reluctance on the part of some teachers to teach these kinds of activities.

Classification of Rhythmic Activities

Classification of activities into certain broad categories is a difficult matter. This is partly due to inconsistencies in the use of terminology to describe certain activities. Thus, any attempt at classification tends to become somewhat of an arbitrary matter and is likely to be based upon experience and personal feelings of the particular person doing the classifying.

When attempts are made to classify activities within a broad category, it should be kept in mind that a certain amount of overlapping is unavoidable and that, in some instances, activities may fit equally well into more than one category. Another important consideration is that in some cases, different names may be given to the same activity, which is concerned with the inconsistencies of terminology mentioned previously. For example, "creative rhythms" and "free-response rhythms" might be considered one and the same.

One approach to the classification of rhythmic activities centers around the kind of *rhythmic experiences* that one might wish children to have. It is recommended here that these experiences consist of (1) unstructured experiences, (2) semistructured experiences, and (3) structured experiences. It should be understood that in this particular way of grouping rhythmic experiences a certain amount of overlapping will occur as far as the degree of structuring is concerned; that is, although an experience is classified as an unstructured one, there could possibly be some small degree of structuring in certain kinds of situations. With this idea in mind the following descriptions of these three types of rhythmic experience is submitted.

Unstructured experiences include those where there is an original or creative response and in which there has been little, if any, previous explanation or discussion in the form of specific directions. The *semistructured experiences* include certain movements or interpretations suggested by the teacher, child, or a group of children. *Structured experiences* involve the more difficult rhythmic patterns associated with various types of dances. A well-balanced program of rhythmic activities for children should provide opportunities for these various types of rhythmic experiences. An arbitrary classification of rhythmic activities designed to provide such experiences for children gives consideration to (1) fundamental rhythms, (2) creative rhythms, (3) movement songs, and (4) dances.

At the primary level, *fundamental rhythmic activities* found in the locomotor movements of walking, running, jumping, hopping, leaping, skipping, galloping, and sliding, and the nonlocomotor or axial movements such as twisting, turning, and stretching, form the basis for all types of rhythmic patterns. Once the children have developed skill in the fundamental rhythms, they are ready to engage in some of the more complex dance patterns. For example, the combination of walking and hopping to musical accompaniment is the basic movement in the aforementioned dance known as the schottischl. In a like manner, galloping is related to the basic pattern used in the polka.

Children at the primary level should be given numerous opportunities to engage in *creative rhythms*. This kind of rhythmic activity helps them to express themselves in just the way the accompaniment "makes them feel" and gives vent to expression so necessary in the life of the child.

The word "creative" derives from the Latin word *creatua,* one meaning of which is "produced through imaginative skill." There may be a slight trend to include more in the way of creative rhythms for children in the modern elementary school. This trend appears to be slight indeed, and as far as the broad area of rhythmic activities is concerned there has been a widespread neglect of creative rhythm for children over the years. This is born out by the various surveys that I have made, which invariably indicate that creative rhythmic experiences for children are provided on a minimal basis.

It is not only unfortunate, but paradoxical, that more widespread use of creative rhythms has not prevailed, given the importance of creativity in the life of the child. Creative experience involves *self*-expression. It is concerned with the need to experiment, to express original ideas, to think, to react. Creativity and childhood enjoy a congruous relationship in that children are naturally creative. They imagine. They pretend. They are uninhibited. They are not only original but actually ingenious in their thoughts and actions. Indeed, creativity is a characteristic inherent in the lives of practically all children, although in various degrees. Some children create as a natural form of expression without adult stimulation, others may need a certain amount of teacher guidance and encouragement.

Such art forms as drawing, music, and writing are traditionally regarded as the best approaches to creative expression. The very essence of creative expression, however, is *movement*. Movement as a form of creativity utilizes the body as the instrument of expression, and especially for the young child this is the most natural form of creative expression. Because of their nature, children have an inclination to movement. It is the child's universal language, a most important form of communication and a most meaningful way of learning.

The *movement song* is a rhythmic activity suitable for primary age children. In this type of activity children can sing their own accompaniment for the various activity patterns that they use in performing the movement song.

Movement songs have traditionally been referred to as *singing games*. This designation, however, is changing, at least in the literature, where there seems to be more of a trend to refer to this form of rhythmic activity as movement songs, and in some cases *action* songs. A reason advanced by Dauer and Pangrazi[3] as to why the term singing games is losing favor in present-day terminology is that few of the songs can accurately be called games.

---

[3]Dauer, Victor P. and Pangrazi, Robert P., *Dynamic Physical Education for Elementary School Children.* 6th ed., Minneapolis, Burgess Publishing Company, 1979, pp. 206–207.

Movement songs have been characterized by Fleming[4] as an initial form of folk dance that has been inherited by children all over the world and is deeply rooted in the heritage of ethnic groups as evidenced by their being danced generation after generation.

Movement songs are actually dances with relatively simple patterns that children perform to their own singing accompaniment or, as the case of recorded accompaniment, when the singing is furnished by others.

Various kinds of *dances* may be included as a part of the program of rhythmic activities for the primary level. Ordinarily, these have simple movement patterns the child may learn before progressing to some of the more complex patterns. At the intermediate level, children can engage in rhythmic activities that are more advanced than those at the primary level. Creative rhythms should be continued, and the children should have the opportunity to create more advanced movement patterns.

Dance patterns involved in the various kinds of folk dances may be somewhat more complex, provided children have had a thorough background in fundamental rhythms and less complicated folk dances at the primary level. Primary level dances can be individual activities and many of them involve dancing with a partner. At the intermediate level, "couple dances," which require closer coordination of movement by partners, may be introduced.

Some of the forms of American square dancing are ordinarily introduced at the intermediate level, although many teachers have had successful experience with square dancing at the lower grade levels.

SELF-TESTING ACTIVITIES

The so-called self-testing activities involve competing against one's self and natural forces. These activities are based upon the child's desire to test his ability in such a way that he attempts to better his own performance. This is a broad term and involves such activities as stunts and tumbling, exercises with or without apparatus, and individual skill proficiency such as throwing for accuracy and/or distance, and jumping for height and distance. Some individuals have resurrected the term *educational gymnastics* to describe these kinds of activities. This term was

---

[4]Fleming, Gladys Andrews, *Creative Rhythmic Movement, Boys and Girls Dancing,* 2nd ed. Englewood Cliffs, NJ, Prentice-Hall, 1976, p. 278.

used around the beginning of this century and was in contrast to the term *medical gymnastics,* which was used to identify activities used to correct certain functional or organic disability or deformity. For purposes here the term *self-testing activities* seems more appropriate to describe this broad category. Moreover, in modern times about 80 percent of the elementary school physical education textbooks use the term self-testing activities while only about 20 percent use the term educational gymnastics.

At the primary level, children should be given the opportunity to participate in self-testing activities that are commensurate with their ability. For example, stunts that involve imitations of animals are of great interest to boys and girls at this age level. Tumbling activities that involve some of the simple rolls are also suitable. Simple apparatus activities involving the use of such equipment as horizontal ladders, low parallel bars, low horizontal bars, and climbing ropes can be utilized.

Self-testing activities at the intermediate level should be somewhat more advanced provided the children have had previous experience and teaching in this type of activity at the primary level. Tumbling activities that involve more advanced rolls and various kinds of body springs may be successfully introduced. Children at the intermediate level may continue to take part in apparatus activities using much the same equipment that was used at the primary level but moving to more advanced skills. When properly taught, apparatus activity is greatly enjoyed and is excellent for muscular development, especially for the torso and arms. Certain basic game skills are sometimes considered self-testing activities and pave the way for competence in a variety of sports. These include throwing for distance and accuracy, soccer kicking and dribbling, and throwing and catching various types of balls.

PART II
COMPENSATORY MOTOR LEARNING

Chapter 4

OVERVIEW

The term *compensatory* as it applies to education is not new, and over the years it has been used in a variety of ways. Possibly its derivation dates back to mid-nineteenth century Denmark.[1] At that time, what was known as the "compensatory education of cripples" involved the teaching of boys and young men with certain physical impairments such skills as basket making and shoe making. The purpose was to prepare people who had certain deformities to make a living on their own.

In this country, at about the turn of the century, it was reported that "by compensatory education for deformed children is meant any special training which will make amends for their physical shortcomings and convert little cripples into men and women better fitted in some one direction to cope with fellow man in the struggle for life."[2]

More recently compensatory education has taken on a much different meaning. That is, it has been concerned essentially with "compensating" for an inadequate early education in some way, or providing a better background for beginning school children who come from a low socioeconomic background. A case in point is the *Headstart* program that has been sponsored by the federal government.

In the early 1970s educators and psychologists in Great Britain attached still a different meaning to compensatory education. In this regard, Morris and Whiting[3] indicated that the term *compensatory education* tended to replace the former term *re-education*. They contended that the term re-education was often misused when standing for compensatory education. Re-education implied educating again persons who had previously reached an educational level and who now, for some reason,

---

[1]The education of crippled children, *American Physical Education Review*, Vol III, No. 3. September 1898, 190–191.

[2]The education of crippled children, *American Physical Education Review*.

[3]Morris, P. R. and Whiting, H. T. A., *Motor Impairment and Compensatory Education*. Philadelphia, Lea & Febiger, 1971, p. 9.

did not exhibit behavior at a level of which they were previously capable. These authors asserted that compensatory education implied an attempt to make good a deficiency in a person's earlier education.

It is from this source that I derived the term *compensatory motor learning*. The rationale for this term is that ordinarily the attempts to improve a deficiency in one's earlier education is likely to take place through the *physical* aspect of the individual's personality. Whereas the standard structured perceptual-motor training programs purport to improve learning ability through systematic exercises and procedures, compensatory motor learning as conceived here, seeks to improve learning ability through participation in motor learning experiences.

Compensatory motor learning attempts to correct various types of child learning disabilities which may stem from an impairment of the central nervous system and/or have their roots in certain social or emotional problems of children. This branch of motor learning, most often through the medium of *perceptual-motor development*, involves the correction, or at least some degree of improvement, of certain motor deficiencies, especially those associated with fine motor coordination. What some specialists have identified as a "perceptual-motor deficit" syndrome is said to exist with certain neurologically handicapped children. An attempt may be made to correct or improve fine motor control problems through a carefully developed sequence of motor competencies which follow a definite hierarchy of development. This may occur through a structured perceptual-motor program which is likely to be dependent upon a series of systematic exercise. Or, it can occur through compensatory motor learning which attempts to provide for these corrections or improvements by having children engage in compensatory motor learning in school physical education activities where perceptual-motor developmental factors may be inherent. This procedure tends to be much more fun for children and at the same time is more likely to be free from emotionally traumatizing situations sometimes attendant in some structured perceptual-motor programs.

The advantage of compensatory motor learning is that it can be incorporated into the regular physical education program rather easily. It can be a part of the function of the physical education teacher, and, with assistance, the classroom teacher can handle many aspects of compensatory motor learning. Or, the regular classroom teacher can conduct such activities independently and on his or her own.

The foregoing statements should not be interpreted as excessive criticism of structured perceptual-motor programs. Under certain conditions, and perhaps particularly in cases of severe neurological dysfunction, such program can be useful. However, caution and restraint in the use of these programs is recommended and they should be conducted under adequate supervision and properly prepared personnel. (Such programs will be discussed briefly later in the chapter.)

PERCEPTUAL-MOTOR DEVELOPMENT

Perception is concerned with how we obtain information from the environment through the various sensory modalities and what we make of it. In the present context *motor* is concerned with the impulse for motion resulting in a change of position through the various forms of body movement. When the two terms are put together (perceptual-motor) the implication is an organization of interpretation of sensory data, with related voluntary motor responses.

Perceptual-Motor Skills

There is a considerable amount of agreement among child development specialists that there is no simple distinction between a perceptual skill and a motor skill. This has, no doubt, led to the term *perceptual-motor skills.* In fact, to some extent this term may have supplanted such terms as *neuromuscular* and *sensorimotor.*

In general, the postulation appears to be that if perceptual training improves perceptual and motor abilities, then, because of the fact that perceptual and motor abilities are so highly interrelated and interdependent upon each other, it follows that training in perception should alleviate perceptual-motor problems. There is objective support for the idea that perception training can improve perceptual ability. Although there is not a great deal of clear-cut evidence to support the idea that perceptual-motor training does increase the performance of perceptual motor skills, some research has indicated that certain perceptual-motor skills can be significantly improved for certain children under certain conditions.

What then are the perceptual-motor skills? Generally, the kinds of skills that fit into a combination of manual coordination and eye-hand skills may be considered a valid classification.

Visual perception is based on sensorimotor experiences that depend on visual acuity, eye-hand coordination, left-right body orientation, and other visual spatial abilities, including visual sequencing. Some studies have shown a positive correlation between difficulties in visual perception and achievement in reading.

Indications of a child's eye-hand coordination may be observed as he bounces or throws a ball, erases a chalkboard, cuts paper with scissors, copies designs, ties his shoelaces, picks up small objects from the floor, or replaces a cap on a pen. It has been indicated that in reading, the child shows difficulty in eye-hand coordination by his inability to keep his place in reading, to find the place again in the pattern of printed words, and to maintain the motor adjustment as long as is necessary to comprehend a word, a phrase, or a sentence. His tendency to skip lines arises from an inability to direct his eyes accurately to the beginning of the next line.

Depending upon a variety of extenuating circumstances, perceptual-motor skills require various degrees of voluntary action. The basic striking and catching skills are examples of this type and are important in certain kinds of active game situations; that is, receiving an object (catching) such as a ball, and hitting (striking) an object, ordinarily with an implement, such as batting a ball. Other kinds of skills in this category, but not related to game activities, include the sorting of objects, finger painting, and bead stringing. There is another group of tasks, perceptual-motor in nature, which involve such factors as choice, discrimination, and problem solving. These may be uncovered by various types of intelligence tests and the ability to perform the tasks under certain conditions.

There are tasks, perceptual-motor in character, that are accomplished with one hand. At a high level of performance this could involve receiving a ball with one hand in a highly organized sports activity such as baseball. At a very low level, a baby will reach for an object or grasp an object with one hand.

In some kinds of visual tasks requiring the use of one eye, there appears to be an eye preference. In reading, it is believed that one eye may lead or be dominant. In tasks where one eye is used and one hand is used, most people will use those on the same side of the body. This is to say that there is *lateral dominance*. In the case of those who use the left eye and right hand or the opposite of this *mixed dominance* is said to exist. Some studies suggest that mixed dominance may have a negative effect on motor coordination, but perhaps just as many investigators report that this is not the case.

A condition often related to dominance as far as reading is concerned is that of *reversals*. One type of reversal (static) refers to a child seeing letters reversed such as *n* and *b* appearing as *u* and *d*. In another type (kinetic) the child may see the word *no* as *on*. At one time reversals were considered as possibly related to dominance. However, later studies tended to negate this earlier view. In more recent years studies tend to support the contention that problems of visual perception, spatial orientation, and recognition of form rather than dominance patterns result in children making reversals.

Perceptual-Motor Programs

Some of the perceptual-motor programs are carried on independently from the school and outside the school situation. However, there are some schools that have acquired the services of a perceptual-motor specialist who operates within the framework of the school physical education program.

In general, perceptual-motor programs fall into the two broad categories of those that are considered to be *structured* and those that are considered to be *unstructured*. Since there are various degrees of structuring in activities making up a given program, a considerable amount of overlapping can exist from one program to another. For example, there can be some degree of structuring in a program that for all practical purposes would be classified as unstructured.

The structured program of perceptual-motor training is based on the notion that some form of physical activity can contribute to the development of a higher learning capacity in children with certain kinds of learning disabilities. The unstructured type of program tends to be more creative in nature and is not so dependent upon a set of more or less "fixed" exercises. Play therapists have been aware of the value of the unstructured type of approach for years, and studies show that through play therapy experiences some changes in reading ability can occur.

Although some attention may be focused upon perceptual-motor programs, it should be made clear that such programs are not a panacea for all the learning problems of children. However, if these types of programs are (1) geared to meet the individual needs of children, (2) remain within the realm of educational objectives, and (3) take into account the development of the child's total personality, they can become an important part of a multidisciplinary approach to some of the learning problems of children.

My review of a large number of studies involving the effect of perceptual-motor programs and/or perceptual-motor activities on academic achievement revealed that about one-third of these were supportive or partially supportive of the procedure while the remaining two-thirds were nonsupportive.

Perhaps the point should be made again that compensatory motor learning seeks to obtain much the same results as those obtained through organized perceptual-motor activities. The essential difference is that compensatory motor learning tends to provide a way of improving learning ability which is free from uninteresting systematic activities. This is to say that the compensatory motor learning experiences are likely to be more motivating and enjoyable.

The development of perceptual-motor abilities in children is referred to by some child development specialists as the process of providing "learning to learn" activities. This means improvement upon such perceptual-motor qualities as *body awareness, laterality,* and *directionality* (sense of direction), *auditory* and *visual perception skills,* and *kinesthetic* and *tactile perception skills.* A deficiency in one or more of these can detract from a child's ability to learn.

It will be the function of the following chapters in Part II to help teachers and others determine if such deficiencies exist, along with recommended compensatory motor learning experiences to help improve upon them. Even though a deficiency does not exist in any of these factors, the motor learning experiences suggested can still be used to sharpen and improve upon these skills which are so important to learning.

Chapter 5

BODY AWARENESS AND MOTOR LEARNING

Communication in this particular area is complicated by a lack of standardization in the use of certain terms. For example, some years ago Brooke and Whiting[1] pointed this up very clearly when they stated that "problems of terminology make this a difficult field for evaluation. . . . The following terms, for example, have been utilized by different writers for the same related concepts: body-schema, body-image, body-awareness, body-concept, body-sense, and body-experience."

It is interesting to note that the term "body awareness" has widespread use among physical educators. This has been my own experience. Also an extensive review of physical education literature on this general subject has revealed that that the term "body awareness" is used much more frequently than other terms. Incidentally, Whiting et al,[2] have given a good definition of body awareness: "an appreciation and understanding of the body as the instrument of movement and vehicle of expression in nonverbal communication."

DETERMINING PROBLEMS OF BODY AWARENESS

It is doubtful that there are any absolutely foolproof methods of detecting problems of body awareness in children. The reason for this is that many mannerisms said to be indicative of body-awareness problems can be symptomatic of other deficiencies. Nevertheless, those persons who are likely to deal in some way with children should be alert to detect certain possible deficiencies.

Generally speaking, there are two ways in which deficiencies concerned with body awareness might be detected. First, some deficiencies can be discerned, at least in part, by observing certain behaviors. And,

[1]Brooke, J. D. and Whiting, H. T. A., *Human Movement: A Field of Study,* London, Henry Kimpton, 1973.

[2]Whiting, H. T., A., et al., *Personality and Performance in Physical Education and Sport,* London, Henry Kimpton, 1973.

second, there are some relatively simple diagnostic techniques which can be used to detect deficiencies. The following generalized list contains examples of both of these possibilities and is submitted to assist the reader in this particular regard.

1. One technique often used to diagnose possible problems of body awareness is to have children make a drawing of themselves. The primary purpose of this is to see if certain parts of the body are *not* included in the drawing. My own personal experience several years ago as a Certified Binet Intelligence Test Examiner revealed possibilities for such a diagnosis inherent in the test item involving *picture completion.* In this test item a partial drawing of a "man" is provided for the child to complete. Since the child's interest in drawing a man dates from his earliest attempts to represent things symbolically, it is possible, through typical drawings of young children, to trace certain characteristic stages of perceptual development. It has also been found that drawing of a picture of himself assists in helping to detect if there is a lack of body awareness. (One of my own experiments concerning this phenomenon is presented later in the chapter.)

2. Sometimes the child with a lack of body awareness may manifest tenseness in his movements. At the same time he may be unsure of his movements as he attempts to move the body segments.

3. Some persons tend to feel that a child with a reversal problem may also have problems with body awareness.

4. If the child is instructed to move a body part such as placing one foot forward, he may direct his attention to the body part before making the movement. Or, he may look at another child to observe the movement before he attempts to make the movement himself. This could be due to poor processing of the input (auditory or visual) provided for the movement.

5. When instructed to use one body part (arm) he may also move the corresponding body part (other arm) when it is not necessary. For example, he may be asked to swing the right arm and he may also start to swing the left arm simultaneously.

6. In such activities as catching an object, the child may turn toward the object when this is not necessary. For example, when a beanbag thrown to him approaches close to the child, he may move forward with either side of the body rather than trying to retrieve the beanbag with his hands while both feet remain stationary.

COMPENSATORY MOTOR LEARNING EXPERIENCES INVOLVING BODY AWARENESS

In general, it might be said that when a child is given the opportunity to use his body freely in enjoyable movement an increase in body awareness occurs. More specifically, there are activities which can be used in helping children identify and understand the use of various body parts as well as the relationship of these parts.

Over a period of years I have conducted a number of experiments in an attempt to determine the effect of participation in certain compensatory learning experiences on body awareness. The following is an example of this quasi-objective approach utilizing the game *Busy Bee.*

In this game the children are in pairs facing each other and dispersed around the activity area. One child who is the *caller* is in the center of the area. He makes calls such as "shoulder-to-shoulder," "toe-to-toe," or "hand-to-hand." (In the early stages of the game it might be a good idea to have the teacher do the calling.) As the calls are made, the paired children go through the appropriate motions with their partners. After a few calls, the caller will shout, "Busy Bee!" This is the signal for every child to get a new partner, including the caller. The child who does not get a partner can become the new caller, or a new caller can be selected by the group.

This game has been experimented with in the following manner:

As the children played the game, the teacher made them aware of the location of various parts of the body in order to develop the concept of full body awareness.

Before the game was played, the children were asked to draw a picture of themselves. Many did not know how to begin, and others omitted some of the major limbs in their drawings. After playing Busy Bee, the children were asked again to draw a picture of themselves. This time they were more successful. All of the drawings had bodies, heads, arms, and legs, Some of them had hands, feet, eyes, and ears. A few even had teeth and hair.

The following compensatory motor learning experiences include those which can be used for diagnosis, body-awareness improvement, evaluation of body-awareness status, or various combinations of these factors. Some of the activities are age-old while others have been developed for specific situations. Some of the activities are in the form of stories which I have developed for the purpose of using compensatory motor learning experiences to improve listening and reading. Each of the activities contains a description of how it is performed along with a statement of suggested application as well as detailing other aspects of the activity.

Everybody Goes

All of the children (except the one who is *It*) stand side by side at one end of the activity area. *It* stands in the middle of the activity area facing the line. At the opposite end of the area there is a goal line. The distance of the playing area can be variable. The game is started with the following rhyme.

Head, shoulders, knees, and toes.
Eyes, ears, mouth, and nose.
Off and running everybody goes.

On the last word "goes," the children in the line run to the other end and try to reach the goal line without being tagged by *It.* All of those tagged become helpers for *It* and the game continues with the children running to the opposite end on the signal. If the game is played in its entirety, *It* continues until there is one player left who can be declared the winner.

As the rhyme is recited, the children in the line do the following motions: head—place both hands on the head; shoulders—place both hands on the shoulders; knees—bend at the waist and place both hands on the knees; toes—bend down and touch the toes and resume standing position; eyes—point to the eyes; ears—point to the ears; mouth—point to the mouth; nose—point to the nose.

Suggested Application: It might be a good idea in the early stages for the teacher to recite the rhyme. The teacher can be the judge of how fast this should be done. The more accomplished the children become, the faster the rhyme can be recited, and the children themselves can recite it in unison. When the game is first played, the teacher can observe closely for those children who are reacting by doing what the rhyme says. It may be found that some are having difficulty. Thus, the activity becomes a means for diagnosing a lack of body awareness. It will be noticed that with practice children will improve in their response to the rhyme. A different form of locomotion can be substituted for *running.* That is, it can be "off and skipping (hopping, jumping, etc.) everybody goes."

Come With Me

Several children form a circle, with one child outside the circle. The child outside the circle walks around it, taps another child and says, "Come with me." The child tapped falls in behind the first child and they continue walking around the circle. The second child taps a child and says, "Come with me." This continues until several children have been tapped. At a given point the first child calls out, "Go home!" On this signal all the children try to get back to their original place in the circle. The first child also tries to get into one of these places. There will be one child left out. He can be the first child for the next game.

Suggested Application: In the early stages the teacher should call out where each child is to be tapped. For example, "on the arm," "on the leg," etc. After a time the child doing the tapping can call out where he is going to tap the child. The teacher can observe if children are tapped in the proper place.

Mirrors

One child is selected as the leader and stands in front of a line of children. This child goes through a variety of different movements and the children in the line try to do exactly the same thing; that is, they act as mirrors. The leader should be changed frequently.

Suggested Application: In this activity the children become aware of different body parts and movements as the child in front makes the various movements. The teacher should be alert to see how well and how quickly the children are able to do the movements that the leader makes.

Move Along

The children lie on their backs on the floor. The teacher gives a signal such as the beat of a drum or clap of the hands and the children move their arms and legs in any way they choose. The teacher then gives the name of a movement such as "Move your legs like a bicycle" and then gives the signal to begin the movement. If the teacher wishes, some sort of scoring system can be devised to reward those children who make the correct movement in the fastest amount of time.

Suggested Application: The teacher should observe closely to see how rapidly the children respond to the movements called. In addition, the teacher should observe to see if some children are waiting to see what others are going to do before making the correct movement.

Change Circles

Several circles are drawn on the floor or outdoor activity area with one less circle than the number of participants. The one child who does not have a circle can be *It* and stands in the middle of the area. The teacher calls out signals in the form of body parts. For example, such calls would include "Hands on knees!" "Hands on head!" "Right hand on your left foot!" and so on. After a time the teacher calls out "Change circles!" whereupon all the children try to get into a different circle while the child who is *It* tries to find a circle. The child who does not find a circle can be *It* or a new person can be chosen to be *It.*

Suggested Application: The teacher should observe closely to see how the children react to the calls and whether or not they are looking at the other children for clues. As time goes on and the children become more familiar with body parts, more complicated calls can be made.

Body Tag

In this activity one child is selected to be *It.* He chases the other children and attempts to tag one of them. If he is successful the child tagged can become *It.* If *It* does not succeed within a reasonable amount of time a new *It* should be selected. In order to be officially tagged, a specific part of the body must be tagged by *It.* Thus, the game could be shoulder tag, or leg tag as desired.

Suggested Application: The teacher observes the child to see whether or not he tags the correct body part. To add more interest to the activity, the teacher can call out the part of the body to be tagged during each session of the game.

Birds Fly South

All of the children except one who is *It* assemble at the end of the activity area. At the other end a goal line is designated. *It* calls out "Birds fly south with hands on knees," or the hands touching any other part of the body. The children take this position as does *It.* They try to run to the opposite end and try to avoid being tagged by *It.* All of those tagged become helpers for *It.* If the game continues in its entirety, all but one player would be tagged. This player can be *It* for next time or a new *It* can be selected.

Suggested Application: The teacher observes whether or not the children assume the correct position before starting to run. If so desired, *It* can call out only the words "Birds fly south" and the teacher can add the name of the body part to be touched. This can add an interesting dimension to the game and give the teacher a greater degree of flexibility in evaluating the performance of the children as far as body awareness is concerned.

Looby Loo

Verse:

1. Here we dance Looby Loo, here we dance Looby Light.
2. Here we dance Looby Loo, all on a Saturday night.
3. I put my right hand in, I take my right hand out.
4. I give my right hand shake, shake, shake, and turn myself about.
> (turn around in place)

I put my left foot in, etc.
I put my right foot in, etc.

Action: The children form a single circle with hands joined. On lines 1 and 2 of the verse the children walk three steps into the circle and three steps back and repeat. As the rest of the lines are sung, the children do actions indicated by the words. For example, with "I put my right hand in," they lean forward, extend the right hand and point it toward the center of the circle. At the end of each verse the children repeat the first verse again, taking three steps in and three steps out. The procedure can be continued with other parts of the body as desired, ending with "I put my whole self in," and so on (Take a short jump in).

Suggested Application: In a discussion before participation in this activity the teacher can be sure the children are aware of the body part and when to activate it. In addition, the activity can serve well as an evaluative device for the teacher to see how well the children are aware of the various body parts.

Diddle Diddle Dumpling

Verse:

1. Diddle Diddle Dumpling, my son John.
2. Went to bed with one shoe on.
3. Yes, one shoe off, and one shoe on.
4. Diddle Diddle Dumpling, my son John.

Action: The children can be in any formation. On the first line they can either clap hands, knees, or thighs, or any other body part. On the second line they can pretend to sleep with motions such as placing their heads on their hands. On the third line they hop on one foot to indicate they have a shoe off. On the fourth line they repeat the action of the first line.

Suggested Application: In a discussion prior to engaging in the activity the teacher and the children can determine which body part is to be clapped and on which foot the shoe will be. During the activity, the teacher can determine easily which children are having difficulty following the instructions.

Big Bee

Verse:

1. Up on toes, back on heels.
2. Hands on head, see how it feels.
3. Bend at the waist, touch your knees.
4. Skip around if you please.
5. Keep on skipping around the ring.
6. Look out for the Big Bee sting.

Action: All the children except the one who is *Big Bee* form a circle. Big Bee stands inside the circle and close to the children in the circle. The children execute the action indicated in the verse as they sing or chant it. On line 4 they skip around the circle clockwise. Big Bee walks around the circle counterclockwise. At the end of the last word of the verse all of the children in the circle stoop down. Big Bee tries to tag (sting) one of the children before that child has assumed the stooping position. A new Big Bee is selected and the activity continues.

Suggested Application: After explaining and discussing the actions that the children are to execute, the extent to which they are able to identify the various body parts concerned can be observed. In evaluating the activity with the children the teacher can ask where a child was *stung*. "On the arm?" "On the leg?" etc.

Clap and Tap

As mentioned previously, some of the activities are presented in story form which have been developed for the purpose of using compensatory motor learning experiences to improve upon listening and reading. *Clap and Tap* is such an activity.

I clap with my hands.
Clap, clap, clap.
I tap with my foot.
Tap, tap, tap.
I point my toe.
And around I go.
Clap, clap, clap.
Tap, tap, tap.

Suggested Application: The teacher can read the story to the children, then during participation the teacher can see how well they follow the body movement directions. The teacher and children can make up their own tune for accompaniment. If the teacher wants to extend the story to the reading task, he or she can give a printed copy to each child. Or, this procedure can be used originally, depending upon the ability of the children.

The Growing Flowers (creative rhythm)

It should be recalled that creative rhythms have already been highly recommended on the basis that when a child is able to use his body freely there is a strong likelihood that there will be increased body awareness. The following is an example of this in story form

Flowers grow.
First they are seeds.
Be a seed.
Grow like a flower.
Grow and grow.
Keep growing.
Keep growing.
Grow tall.
Now you are a flower.

Suggested Application: The teacher can carefully observe the movements of the children with reference to the body parts used in the growing flowers. "Did we use our arms?" "Our legs?" and so on. A drum or suitable recording can be used as accompaniment if desired.

Measuring Worm

The child extends his body along the surface area in a straight line, face down. His weight is supported by his hands and toes. With arms and legs extended he takes very short steps until his feet reach his hands. He then moves ahead on his hands with very short "steps" until his body is extended again. He continues to do this for a specified distance.

Suggested Application: It should be brought to the attention of the child how he is using his hands and feet to move along like a measuring worm. In discussing this activity with children, the uses of the body parts, hands, arms, feet, and legs are considered. During the activity the teacher can see how each child reacts to directions. Sometimes children confuse hands and arms and feet and legs.

Spanker

The child lies on his back and raises his body by pushing up with his feet and hands. He walks along in this position on hands and feet. He raises first one hand and then the other as he taps (spanks) himself.

Suggested Application: The hands and feet are identified in terms of their coordinated use. As the child becomes more proficient in the activity the teacher can give instructions to *spank* the body in different places, such as thighs, head, etc.

Squat Thrust

From a standing position the child assumes a squatting stance, placing his hands on the surface area to the outside of his legs with the palms flat and the fingers forward. This count is number 1. Switching the weight to the hands and arms, then the child extends his legs sharply to the rear until his body is straight. The weight of the body is now on the hands and the balls of the feet. This count is number 2. On count number 3 the child returns to the squatting position, and on count number 4 the child returns to the erect standing position.

Suggested Application: The child is able to see the function of certain body parts as the weight is shifted. After directions are given for the performance of the activity the teacher can notice how well they are followed with reference to the correct position of the body parts concerned.

Turk Stand

The Turk Stand may be presented in story form as follows.

The Little King
In a faraway land across the sea lives a Little King.
This Little King stands straight and tall.

He folds his arms in front of him.
He crosses one foot in front of the other.
He sits down slowly.
Now the Little King wants to get up.
He keeps his arms the same way.
He rises in this way.
Now he stands straight again.

Suggested Application: The teacher can observe how well the children execute the movement after listening to the story, and thus use it as a diagnostic technique.

Chapter 6

LATERALITY AND DIRECTIONALITY
AND MOTOR LEARNING

L aterality and directionality are concerned with distinction of the body sides and sense of direction. More specifically, laterality is an internal awareness of the left and right sides of the body in relation to the child himself. It is concerned with the child's knowledge of how each side of the body is used separately or together. Directionality is the projection into space of laterality; that is, the awareness of left and right, up and down, over and under, etc. in the world around the child. Stated in another way, directionality in space is the ability to project outside the body the laterality that the child has developed within himself.

The categories of laterality and directionality make up the broader classification of *directional awareness*. The development of this quality is most important, in that it is an essential element for reading and writing. These two basic Rs require the hand and/or eyes to move from left to right in a coordinated manner. Also, interpretation of left and right direction is an important requirement for the child in dealing with the environment. It is interesting to note that some children who have *not* developed laterality quite often will write numbers sequentially from left to right. However, when doing addition and subtraction, they may want to start from the left instead of the right. Compensatory motor learning experiences designed to differentiate right from left sides of the body are an important part of remedial arithmetic.

DETERMINING PROBLEMS OF
LATERALITY AND DIRECTIONALITY

Since laterality and directionality are inherent aspects of body awareness, some of the methods for detecting deficiencies in body awareness mentioned previously also apply here. In addition, it may be noted that the child is inclined to use just the dominant side of his body. Also, confusion may result if the child is given directions for body movement which call for a specific direction in which he is to move.

In activities that require a child to run to a given point such as a base, he may tend to veer away from it. Or, he may not perceive the position of other children in a game, and, as a consequence, may run into them frequently. These are factors that teachers can observe in children in their natural play environment, or in their movements in the classroom.

Some teachers have indicated that they have had success with a specific test of laterality. This test is given on a four-inch-wide walking board which is two feet in length. The child tries to walk forward, backward, and sideways, right to left and left to right, while attempting to maintain his balance. It is suggested that a child with laterality problems will experience difficulty moving one of the ways sideward, ordinarily from left to right.

COMPENSATORY MOTOR LEARNING EXPERIENCES INVOLVING LATERALITY AND DIRECTIONALITY

Generally speaking, a relatively large number of compensatory motor learning experiences involve some aspect of lateralness, while a more moderate number are concerned with directionality. Some motor learning activities involve *unilateral* movements; those performed with one side or part of the body. Many motor learning activities provide *bilateral* movement. This means that both sides or segments of the body are in action simultaneously in the same manner. *Cross-lateral* movement is involved when segments of the body are used simultaneously but in a different manner. Many activities are concerned with changing direction which is likely to involve directionality. The activities that follow have been selected because they contain certain inherent experiences in laterality and/or directionality. Also, in some of the activities, these inherent experiences are more pronounced and receive more emphasis than might be the case with certain other activities.

Zigzag Run

The group is divided into teams. The teams form rows behind a starting line. Four ten pins, or other objects, are placed in a line four feet apart in front of each team. On a signal, the first child on each team runs to the right of the first pin and to the left of the second pin, and so on, in a zigzag fashion, going around the last pin. He returns to place in the same manner. The second child proceeds as the first child. If a child knocks down a pin, he must set it up before he continues. The team finishing first wins.

Suggested Application: This activity gives children practice in changing direction as they run around the objects. The teacher can observe closely to notice the children who are having difficulty performing the task.

Circle Run

In this activity the players form a circle and stand about six feet apart. All face counterclockwise. On a signal, all start to run, keeping the general outline of the circle. As they run, each player tries to pass the runner in front of him on the outside. A player passing another tags the one passed and the one passed is out of the race. The last person left in the circle wins. On a designated signal from the teacher the circle turns around and runs in a clockwise direction. This may occur at the discretion of the teacher. (As a general policy, children should not be eliminated from an activity; however, this is a strenuous, rapid-moving activity and a player is soon back in the game because of the short playing time.)

Suggested Application: Signals the teacher can use for changing direction are *forward* and *backward* or *front* and *back*. The teacher can observe those children who react slowly to the directions and how quickly they make the change after they do react. This is a good activity for helping children identify the words that mean a change in direction from front to back.

Corn Race

This is a modern version of a game that goes back into the history of our country. In early times while adults were husking corn the children played games with the ears of corn. The group is divided into a number of rows. In front of each row a circle about three feet in diameter is drawn on the playing surface to represent a corn basket. Straight ahead beyond each of the corn baskets, four smaller circles are drawn about ten feet apart. In each of the four small circles is placed an object representing an ear of corn. These objects may be blocks, beanbags or the like. At a signal, the first child in each row runs to the small circles in front of, and in line with his row, picks up the corn, one ear at a time, and puts all the ears into the corn basket. The second child takes the ears from the corn basket and replaces them in the small circles. The third child picks them up and puts them in the basket, and the game proceeds until all members have run and returned to their places.

Suggested Application: This activity provides an opportunity to move forward and backward and to place objects in the process. The teacher should take note of those children who may be confused about their particular task. Assistance can be given to those children who need it, either by the teacher or by other children.

Go and Stop

The children stand in dispersed fashion around the activity area with one person designated as the leader. The leader points in a given direction and says, "Hop that way." Or the leader may say, "Skip to the wall." When the leader calls out, "Stop!" all of the children must stoop down. The idea is to not be the last one down. The last child down has a point scored against him and the game continues for a specified period of time.

Suggested Application: In the early stages of this game it might be a good idea for the teacher to be the leader so that the various calls can be controlled. The teacher can observe those children who are able to go immediately in the direction the leader specifies. The teacher should be on the alert to watch for those children who look at another child before making a movement. This can suggest that these children are having difficulty following directions.

Ostrich Tag

The children are dispersed around the activity area. One child selected to be *It* attempts to tag one of the children who may protect himself from being tagged by standing in ostrich fashion. That is, he may stand on one foot with his hands behind his back to emulate an ostrich. The other leg is swung back and forth to help maintain balance. If *It* tags a child before he is in this position or after he has moved, that child becomes *It.*

Suggested Application: Before the game starts the teacher can indicate to the children on which foot they are to stand. The teacher can then take note if they are standing on the designated foot. The teacher might also take note of those children who are having difficulty in maintaining balance when standing on one foot.

Changing Seats

Enough chairs for all the children in the group are placed side by side in about four or five rows. The children sit alert, ready to move either way. The teacher calls, "Change right!" and each child moves into a seat on his right. When the teacher calls, "Change left!" each child moves left. The child at the end of the row who does not have a seat to move to must run to the other end of his row to sit in the vacant seat there.

Suggested Application: The teacher can bring excitement to the game by the quickness of commands or unexpectedness by calling the same direction several times in succession. After each signal the first row of children who all find seats may score a point for that row. This is a good activity to help the children learn the distinction between right and left and to listen to the terms that designate the direction. The teacher should observe those children who move in the wrong direction on signal. Special attention should be given by the teacher when the same signal is called several times in succession. By this careful observation, it can be determined whether or not certain children actually know the directions or are guessing which signal the teacher will give.

Over and Under Relay

The children form several rows, an equal number in each. The first child in each row is given a ball or other object that can be passed to the children behind. At a signal the first child hands the object over his head to the second child; the second child passes it between his legs to the third child; and the third child passes it over his head, etc. When the last child receives the object, he runs to the head of his row and the same procedure is followed. This procedure continues until the first child returns to the head of his row. The row first completing the circuit wins the game.

Suggested Application: This activity gives the children an opportunity to pass an object in a backward direction while at the same time changing direction. The teacher can have the children call out "over" or "under" as the case may be so that they can become familiar with the meaning. The terminology can be changed to "up" and "down" if the teacher so desires.

Change Circle Relay

The group is arranged in rows. Three circles are drawn on the surface area a given distance in front of each row. In the circle to the left of each row three objects are placed. These objects can be ten pins or anything that can be made to stand upright. The first child runs to the circle and moves the objects to the next circle; the second child moves them to the last circle, and then each succeeding child repeats this process. That is, the objects are moved from the first circle to the second circle to the third circle, and then back to the first circle. All of the objects must remain standing. If one falls, the last child to touch it must return and set it up. The activity is complete when all the players on a team have had an opportunity to change the objects from one circle to another.

Suggested Application: The number of objects can be varied and the activity can be started with just one object. This activity gives the children an opportunity to execute change in direction by placing objects in specified places. If the teacher desires, the circles can be labeled with *left, center,* and *right.*

Hickory Dickory Dock

Verse:

1. Hickory Dickory Dock.
2. The mouse ran up the clock.
3. The clock struck one!
4. Watch the mouse run!
5. Hickory Dickory Dock.

Action. The children form a double circle with partners facing. On line 1 the hands are in front of the body to form a pendulum and the arms are swung left and right. On line 2 partners change places with six short running steps. On line 3 they clap hands over head. On line 4 they go back to their original place with six short running steps. On line 5 they swing the arms as in line 1.

Suggested Application: The teacher should observe the smoothness of the arm movements as the children swing the arms and whether or not the children are following directions. After line 2 the position of the children should be noted to make sure that they have made the correct movement. Certain words such as *up,* can be emphasized as directional terms.

How Do 'Ye Do, My Partner

Verse

1. How do'ye do, my partner.
2. How are you today?
3. Shall we dance in a circle?
4. I will show you the way.
5. Tra, la, la, la, la, la, etc (chorus)

Action: The following actions are performed with the singing accompaniment. A double circle is formed, girls on the outside and boys on the inside. Partners face each other and bow. Partners join inside hands and skip counterclockwise around the circle during the chorus. On the last two measures of the chorus the boys move ahead one person and continue to dance with a new partner.

Suggested Application: Each child gets an opportunity to skip with a partner in a given direction. The teacher should observe closely for those boys who do not move forward to the new partner at the proper time. They must coordinate the timing of the verse with the appropriate time to move ahead one person.

A-Hunting We Will Go

Verse

1. Oh! a-hunting we will go.
2. A-hunting we will go.
3. We'll find a fox and put him in a box.
4. But then we'll let him go.

Action: Either four or six children stand in two lines, partners facing each other. The two partners nearest the front of the area should be designated as the head couple. The head couple joins hands and slides four steps down away from the front of the room between the two lines while singing the first line of the verse. The other children clap and sing the accompaniment. On line 2 the head couple slides four steps back to their original position. The head couple then drops hands and the head girl skips around to the right and to the end of her line. The head boy does the same thing to his left. This is done while singing lines 3 and 4. They both meet at the other end of the line. The new head couple follows this procedure and then all succeeding couples become head couples until everyone has had an opportunity to be the head couple.

After each couple has been the head couple, the children all join hands and circle clockwise while singing the entire verse.

Suggested Application: The children who clap and sing the accompaniment must coordinate their tempo with those who are sliding, and vice versa. The children who slide have an opportunity to change direction in a lateral plane upon the auditory clue. The teacher can be on the alert to notice those children who are following directions correctly.

Children's Polka

In the starting position for this dance the children form a single circle. Partners turn and face each other. They join hands and extend the arms to shoulder height. A number of suitable recordings are available for this dance.

Accompaniment Action

Measures 1–2: Partners take two slides toward the center of the circle and stamp feet three times in place—right, left, right.

Measures 3–4: Partners take two slides back to original position and stamp feet three times.

Measures 5–8: Repeat the action in Measures 1–4.

Measures 9–10: Clap hands against own thighs, clap own hands, and clap partner's hands three times.

Measures 11–12: Repeat the action in Measures 9–10.

Measure 13: Extend the right foot to the side with the toe down. Hold the right elbow in the left hand and shake the right forefinger at partner three times.

Measure 14: Same as Measure 13 except that the position is reversed with the left foot and left hand.

Measure 15–16: Each person turns around with four running steps and then stamps feet three times—right, left, right.

Suggested Application: This dance provides many opportunities for the children to change directions while at the same time performing a coordinated movement with the hands, such as clapping one's own hands and the partner's hands. As the children learn the activity, the teacher can stress the terms *right* and *left* since they are used for directions for sliding. In all structured rhythmic activities such as those preceding, the teacher might take note of those children who are depending upon others for directions. This could indicate that these children are having more pronounced problems of laterality and/or directionality. Thus, structured rhythmic activities can serve as a diagnostic technique.

Ball-Handling Activities

Ball-handling activities can be useful in helping children develop eye-hand coordination, timing, and bilaterality. The following list of activities is concerned with all of these factors in some way.

Stationary Bounce. Using both hands, bounce the ball to the surface area and catch it while standing in place. This can be repeated any number of times.

Walking Bounce. Using both hands, bounce the ball to the surface area and catch it while walking.

Partner Bounce. Using both hands, bounce the ball to a partner who returns it. The distance between the partners can be increased as desired.

Bounce Around. Children form a circle; using both hands, they bounce the ball around the circle, with each child retrieving it and bouncing it to the next child. The circle can be made up of any number of children; however, not more than five are recommended, so that each child will get the greatest number of turns.

Stationary Tap. Tap the ball with one hand while standing in place. Either hand can be used depending upon the individual child, and the tapping can be repeated any number of times.

Throw and Catch. Throw the ball into the air and catch it. The height of the throw can be increased as desired.

Bounce-Clap-Catch. Bounce the ball to the surface area and clap the hands before catching it.

Balance Beam Activities

Generally speaking, there are two classifications of balance beams: the *high* balance beam and the *low* balance beam. The high balance beam, although adjustable, is ordinarily placed at a height of four feet from the surface area. The width of the high balance beam is four inches. The high balance beam is considered to be the official beam for higher-level gymnastic competition.

The low balance beam is ordinarily six to ten inches above the surface area and the width of the beam is two inches. When a four-inch width is used at this height it is generally referred to as a *walking board.* This greater width is often desirable when young children are beginning to learn balance beam activities. All of the discussions here and the activities that will follow are concerned only with the low balance beam.

There are two types of balance; that is, *static* balance and *dynamic* balance. Static balance is the retention of balance in a stationary position and dynamic balance is the ability to maintain balance during body movement. We are predominantly concerned here with dynamic balance.

Two important factors need to be considered as general procedures employed in the teaching of balance beam activities. These are *mounting* and *spotting*. In a very large majority of cases the lack of success in balance beam activities is due to the fact that the child mounts the beam incorrectly. The incorrect but usual procedure is that the child stands in front of the beam, instead of standing in the correct mounting position *astride* the beam. When a child stands in front of the beam, he must shift his weight forward rather than sideward and thus mounts the beam in an "off-balance" position. Standing astride the beam, the child places his foot on the beam and then shifts his weight sideward before releasing the opposite foot from the surface area. With this procedure, it is much easier to maintain balance while mounting the beam.

There is a tendency for many teachers to *spot* or assist the child from the side rather than from the front or rear. When the *spotter* walks along at the side of the child and holds his hand, there appears to be a psychological tendency for the child to lean in that direction, whether he needs assistance or not. This can cause him to lose his balance. For this reason, if the child needs assistance, it is more helpful to him if the spotter walks behind him with his hands on the child's waist, or in front of him holding his hands. The same situation holds true if the balance beam is close to the wall for the purpose of the child using the wall for support. The psychological tendency seems to prevail and the child tends to lean toward the wall. Moreover, the child can inadvertently push away from the wall, causing the balance beam to slide and exposing the child to injury.

The following low balance beam activities are representative of many possibilities suitable for use with children. These activities help the child maintain his relationship to gravity and at the same time help him to develop space awareness and directionality-related movements.

Front Walk. Walk forward on the beam using any length of step.

Back Walk. Walk backward on the beam using any length of step.

Front and Back Walk. Walk forward to the center of the beam using any length step; turn and continue, walking backward, using any length of step to the end of the beam.

Forward Foot Front Walk. Walk forward on the beam with either foot always in front of the other. The lead foot moves forward and the trailing foot comes up to the lead foot but not beyond it.

Backward Foot Back Walk. Walk backward on the beam with either foot always in the lead.

Front Walk Retrieve Object. Place an object such as a chalkboard eraser or book in the center of the beam. Walk forward, stoop down, pick up the object and continue walking to the end of the beam before dismounting.

Front Walk Kneel. Walk forward to the center of the beam, kneel down until one knee touches the beam, rise to an upright position and continue walking to the end of the beam.

Front Walk Object Balance. Place an object on the head. Mount the beam and walk the length of the beam while balancing the object on the head.

Back Walk Object Balance. Place an object on the head. Mount the beam and walk backwards the length of the beam while balancing the object on the head.

Front Walk Retrieve and Balance Object. Place an object in the center of the beam. Walk forward to the center of the beam, stoop down and pick up the object, place it on the head, and continue walking to the end of the beam while balancing the object.

Front Walk Over. Have two children hold a piece of string or rope stretched across the center of the beam at a height of about 12 to 15 inches. Walk forward on the beam, step over the string and continue walking to the end of the beam.

Back Walk Over. The same procedure is used as for the Front Walk Over, except that the child walks backward on the beam.

Front Walk Under. Have two children hold a piece of string or rope stretched across the center of the beam at a height of about three or four feet. Walk forward on the beam, stoop down and go under the string, and then continue walking to the end of the beam.

Back Walk Under. The same procedure is used as for the Front Walk Under, except that the child walks backward on the beam.

Stunts and Tumbling

Stunts have been described as certain kinds of imitations and the performance of a variety of feats that utilize such abilities as balance, coordination, flexibility, agility, and strength. Tumbling involves various kinds of body rolls and body springs that encourage the development of these same abilities. The following activities are representative of those that can be used for the improvement of laterality and directionality.

Crab Walk. The child sits on the surface area with his knees bent and his hands on the surface area behind his hips. He raised his hips until his trunk is straight. In this position he walks forward and backward or to the side.

Suggested Application: The number of steps taken may be specified with reference to direction. That is, so many steps forward and so many steps backward. Also, the teacher can call out the directions for the "crab" to pursue: forward, backward, or sideward left or right.

Rocking Chair. Two children sit facing each other, with feet close to the body. Each sits on the feet of the other. They grasp each other just above the elbows and, in this position, rock back and forth.

Suggested Application: The child can call out the words *forward* and *back* as they rock.

Up and Down. Two children stand facing each other holding hands. One child stoops down. When he stands, the other stoops down.

Suggested Application: They can go up and down any number of times, each time calling out whether they are up or down.

Wicket Walk. The child walks forward and backward or to the side on all fours. The hands are kept flat on the surface area and the knees are straight. The hands are placed far enough apart in the front of the feet so that the knees do not bend.

Suggested Application: Directions for the movement can be given by the teacher or by other children. When children give the directions, they can observe the change in direction of other children.

Log Roll. The child assumes an extended prone position with his stomach facing the mat. The extended body position along the vertical axis is accomplished by placing the arms over the head along the mat until they are straight. The legs are also extended with the feet together and the toes pointed. The child then uses his head, shoulders, and hips to turn 360 degrees along the mat.

Suggested Application: The child should attempt to roll in a straight line in either direction down the mat. This is a good activity for developing directional movement. The teacher should observe those children who are not rolling in a straight line. This can be improved by keeping the body extended and straight. The child can call out his own movements as he rolls first to one side and then to the other.

Forward Roll. The child assumes a squatting position, his hands placed on the mat, palms flat and fingers forward, a shoulder-width apart. The knees are between the arms, the neck is flexed, and the chin should be close to the chest. The initial movement is given to the body by an extension of the ankle joint so the force is extended at the balls of the feet. This forward motion moves over the arms and hands as the head is lowered and the buttocks raised. The arms are closely bent in order to allow the head to move under the hips without touching the mat. The nape of the neck will come in contact with the mat first, and then the momentum will be transferred to the back, moving, respectively, to the buttocks and to the feet. The body should retain the tuck position throughout the activity, and the child should not allow his hands to touch the mat after the original placement at the starting position.

Suggested Application: This is a good movement for bilaterality and directionality. If the child continually rolls over his shoulders, have him move his legs to the outside of his elbows and place the hands a little more than a shoulder-width apart. Instruct children who have difficulty to spread their feet as far apart as possible to perform the roll. Children who need help can be assisted by the teacher lifting them at the nape of the neck and at the shin of the leg.

Backward Roll. The child assumes the starting position by squatting on the feet, which are approximately a shoulder-width apart. He places his hands, palms up, tightly above his shoulders and keeps his elbows in front of his chest. His thumbs are pointed toward his ears and his fingers pointed backward. If possible, the chin touches the chest. Momentum is created by a loss of the equating balance backward (push with the balls of the feet). The tuck position is maintained as the buttocks, back, hands, and feet, respectively, come in contact with the mat. Arms are straightened at the point where the shoulders and hands touch the mat and the buttocks are over the mat. The activity ends with the child on his feet, back in the initial squatting position.

Suggested Application: The child can be assisted by lifting under and grasping each side of his hips. For the child who has difficulty, have him assume a position on his back and place his hands on the mat as if he were doing the roll. Then have him spread his legs apart and reach over his head with his legs until his toes touch the mat. Next, pick him up under his hips to give him the "feel" of the activity.

Chapter 7

IMPROVING FORMS OF PERCEPTION
THROUGH MOTOR LEARNING

In view of the fact that Chapter 7 deals with sensory modalities that modify the term *perception,* it seems appropriate to mention again that perception is concerned with how we obtain information from the environment through the various sensory modalities and what we make of it.

According to the late world famous learning theorist, Jean Piaget, perception is developmental and it changes with age and experience. Development of perception occurs in three major periods: (1) sensorimotor intelligence, which occurs during the period from birth to about two years, is concerned with learning to coordinate various perceptions and movements; (2) the ages from two to about 11 or 12 involve preparation for and organization of concrete operations, and deal with the acquisition of language (it is during this period that the child learns to deal logically with his surroundings); and (3) the formal operations that occur after the age of 11 or 12, and deal with the development of abstract and formal systems.

Learning theorists agree that the senses most involved in learning are *kinesthetic* perception, *tactile* perception, *visual* perception, and *auditory* perception. These are the topics for discussion in this final chapter of Part II.

KINESTHETIC PERCEPTION

Kinesthesis, the kinesthetic sense, has been described in many ways. Some definitions of the term are somewhat comprehensive while others are less so. One comprehensive definition of kinesthesis is that it is the sense which enables us to determine the position of the segments of the body, their rate, extent, and direction of movement, the position of the entire body, and the characteristics of total body motion. Another, less complicated description of the terms characterizes it as the sense that tells the individual where his body is and how it moves.

In summarizing the many definitions of the term the following four factors seem to be constant, thus emphasizing the likenesses of the many definitions of the term: (1) position of the body segments, (2) precision of movement, (3) balance, and (4) space orientation. For the discussion here I will think of kinesthetic perception as the *mental interpretation of the sensation of body movement.*

Although there are a number of specific test items that are supposed to measure kinesthesis, the use of such tests may be of questionable value in diagnosing deficiencies in young children. Therefore, my recommendation is that teachers and others resort to the observation of certain behaviors and mannerisms of children, using some simple diagnostic techniques to determine deficiencies in kinesthetic sensitivity.

Various authorities on the subject suggest that children with kinesthetic problems possess certain characteristics that may be identifying factors. For example, it has been indicated that a child who is deficient in kinesthetic sensitivity will likely be clumsy, awkward, and inefficient in his movements and impaired in getting acquainted with the handling the world of objects. A child who has difficulty in the use of his hands or his body in attempting to perform unfamiliar tasks involving body movement can no doubt benefit from activities involving kinesthesis.

With reference to the above, teachers and others should be on the alert to observe a child who has difficulty with motor coordination; that is, using the muscles in such a manner that they work together effectively. Such lack of coordination may be seen in children who have difficulty in performing the movement skills that involve an uneven rhythm such as *skipping.* Teachers can observe these deficiencies in the normal movement activities of children, and a skill such as skipping can be used as a diagnostic technique in identifying such problems. (Recall that the skill of skipping was discussed in Chapter 2.)

Since balance is an important aspect of kinesthesis, simple tests for balance can be administered to determine if there is a lack of proficiency. One such test is to have the child stand on either foot. Ordinarily, a child should be able to maintain such a position for a period of at least five seconds.

TACTILE PERCEPTION

The tactile sense is very closely related to the kinesthetic sense; so much so, in fact, that these two senses are often confused. One of the main reasons for this is that the ability to detect changes in touch (tactile) involves many of the same receptors concerned with informing the body of changes in its position. The essential difference between the tactile sense and the kinesthetic sense may be seen in the definitions of kinesthetic and tactile perception. As stated previously, kinesthetic perception involves the mental interpretation of the sensation of movement whereas tactile perception is concerned with the *mental interpretation of what a person experiences through the sense of touch.*

Since the kinesthetic and tactile senses are so closely related, the identifying factors of deficiency in kinesthesis previously reported can also be used to determine if there is a deficiency in the tactile sense. Also, a number of elementary diagnostic techniques for tactile sensitivity can be played in a passive game-type situation so that the child is unaware of being tested. The following list suggests some representative examples, and creative teachers are limited only by their own imagination in expanding the list.

1. Have the child explore the surface and texture of objects around the room. Determine if he can differentiate among these objects.
2. Evaluate the child's experience by having him give the names of two or three hard objects, two or three rough objects, and so on.
3. Make a *touching box* by using an ordinary shoebox. Place several differently-shaped objects and differently-textured objects in the box. Have the child reach into the box without looking, and have him feel the various objects to see if he can identify them.

COMPENSATORY MOTOR LEARNING EXPERIENCES INVOLVING KINESTHETIC PERCEPTION

Since kinesthetic sensitivity is concerned with the sensation of movement and orientation of the body in space, it is not an easy matter to isolate specific activities suited *only* for this purpose. The reason for this, of course, is that practically all of these activities involve total or near total physical response. However, activities that make the child particularly aware of the movement of certain muscle groups, as well as those where he encounters resistance, are of particular value in helping the child develop a kinesthetic awareness of his body.

Rush and Tug

In this activity there are two groups with each group standing between one of two parallel lines which are about 40 feet apart. In the middle of these two parallel lines is a rope laid perpendicular to them. A cloth is tied to the middle of the rope to designate both halves of the rope. On a signal, members of both groups rush to their half of the rope, pick it up and tug toward the group's end line. The group pulling the midpoint of the rope past its own end line in a specified amount of time is the winner. If, at the end of the designated time, the midpoint of the rope has not been pulled beyond either group's line, the group with the midpoint of the rope nearer to its end line is the winner.

Suggested Application. In this game the children should be reminded of the resistance they are experiencing as they try to pull the opposing group; also, the experience of feeling the muscle groups of the arms and legs working together.

Poison

The players form a circle and join hands. A circle is drawn on the activity area inside the circle of players and about 12 to 18 inches in front of the feet of the circle of players. With hands joined they pull and tug each other, trying to make one or more persons step into the drawn circle. Anyone who steps into the circle is said to be "Poisoned." As soon as a person is poisoned, someone calls out "Poison!" and the one who is poisoned becomes *It* and gives chase to the others. The other players run to various objects of certain material designated as *safety*, such as wood, stone, metal, and the like. All of the players tagged are poisoned and become chasers. After those not tagged reach safety, the leader calls out "Change!" and they must run to another safety point. Those tagged attempt to tag as many others as possible. The game can continue until all but one have been poisoned.

Suggested Application. This activity provides an opportunity for kinesthetic awareness as a child tries to keep from being pulled into the circle. Also, surface area resistance may be encountered depending upon the type of surface where the activity takes place.

Rhythmic Activity Stories

Practically all rhythmic activities are useful in the improvement of kinesthetic sensitivity. However, there are certain types of rhythmic activities that can make the child aware of the movements of certain muscle groups. I have developed specific rhythmic activities in the form of stories for the purpose of using the compensatory motor learning experience to improve listening and reading. Two of these stories are presented here and emphasize the movement of certain muscle groups. The child is alerted to this because the story gives him directions for the movements to be made.

We Dance

We hold hands.
We make a ring.
We swing our arms.
We swing.
We swing.
We take four steps in.
We take four steps out.
We drop our hands.
We turn about.

Around the Ring

Do you know a song about hunting?
It is called, "A–Hunting We Will Go."
Here is one way to do it.
Children hold hands in a ring.
Sing these words.
Sing them like you would sing.
"A–Hunting We Will Go."
Oh! Around the ring we go.
Around the ring we go.
We stop right here.
We clap our hands.
And then sit down just so.

Suggested Application. The teacher can evaluate the experience with the children by questioning them about what they did. Also, the activities can be repeated to see if the children show improvement in understanding the muscle groups involved in the performance of the activities.

Ball Handling Activities

The use of different-sized balls are of value as far as *timing* relates to kinesthetic perception. In addition to those described in Chapter 6, the following are of value.

Bounce-Turn-Catch. Bounce the ball and turn around and catch it before it bounces a second time. At the outset of this activity, it may be a good idea to throw the ball into the air, then turn around to catch it on the bounce. In this variation, the child has more time to turn around before the ball bounces.

Leg-Over Bounce. Bounce the ball, swing the leg over it, and catch it. This can be done with either leg, and then the legs can be alternated.

Leg-Over Tap. This is the same as the Leg-Over Bounce except the child causes the ball to bounce by continuous tapping.

Wall Target Throw. Throw the ball at a wall target, catching it when it returns. The distance can be increased and the size of the target decreased as desired.

Balance Beam Activities

As mentioned previously, balance beam activities are an extremely important factor in kinesthesis. Along with those already described, the following may also be used to advantage in improving kinesthetic sensitivity.

Front Walk Kneel with Leg Extension. Walk forward to the center of the beam and kneel down until one knee touches the beam. From this position, extend the opposite leg forward until the leg is straight and the heel of the extending leg is touching the beam. Return to the upright position on the beam and continue walking to the end of the beam.

Back Walk Kneel with Leg Extension. The same procedure is used as for the Front Walk Kneel with Leg Extension, except that the child walks backward on the beam.

COMPENSATORY MOTOR LEARNING EXPERIENCES INVOLVING TACTILE PERCEPTION

Electric Shock

The players form a circle with one player designated as *It* standing inside the circle. *It* attempts to determine where the *electric power* is concentrated. The players in the circle join hands and one player is designated to start the electricity. This player accomplishes this by tightly squeezing the hand of the person next to him. As soon as a person's hand is squeezed, he keeps the electricity moving by squeezing the hand of the person next to him. If *It* thinks he knows where the electric power is—that is, whose hand is being squeezed—he calls out that person's name. If *It* has guessed correctly, all of the players in the circle run to a previously designated safety area to avoid being tagged by him. A point is scored against all of those tagged and the game continues with another player becoming *It.*

Suggested Application. In this situation, the tactile sense becomes a medium of communication as each child's hand is squeezed by another, and this method of signalling can be brought to the attention of the children.

Feel and Pass

The children form a circle and face outward with their hands behind them. Articles that have a particular textural characteristic are held by a designated person and passed around the circle from one child to another behind their backs so that they cannot see the articles. One child designated as the last person in the circle receives all the articles and places them in a container in the order he received them. The children then attempt to describe the articles in the order received by them.

Suggested Application. After the game is played with one circle, there can be several small circles and the articles can be passed to see which circle finishes first. Additional articles can be added as the children gain more proficiency in tactility. The activity can serve as a diagnostic technique since the teacher can note the children who cannot identify the articles correctly.

Fish Net

The children are divided into two groups. One group is the net; the other is the fish. At the start, the groups stand behind two goal lines at the opposite ends of the activity area, facing each other. When the teacher gives a signal, both groups run forward toward the center. The net tries to catch as many fish as possible by making a circle around them by holding hands. The fish try to get out of the opening until the hands are joined again. The fish are safe if they get to the opposite goal line without being caught in the net. When the net has made its circle, the number of fish inside are counted and the score is recorded. The next time the groups change places.

Suggested Application. The children get the *feel* of working together as a group with hands joined. The teacher should help them to see the need for keeping the net intact by holding hands firmly.

Join Hands Relay

Several relay teams form behind the starting line. The first member of each team stands on the opposite goal line, a given distance away, facing his relay team. At the signal to start, this first member runs to the second member of his team, takes him by the hand and together they run to the goal line. The first member remains there and the second member returns to bring back the third member. This procedure is continued until all members have reached the goal line. The winner is the first full team to arrive at the goal line.

Suggested Application. It might be a good idea to arrange the children in such a way that they are nearly equal in running speed. That is, the purpose could be defeated if a very fast and a very slow runner were teamed up. The children must cooperate in running back to the goal line with hands joined, and thus they see and feel the importance of running together well for the success of the entire team.

Chain Tag

One child is chosen as leader. The leader chooses another child to assist him and the two join hands. They chase the other children, trying to tag one. When a child has been tagged, he takes his place between the two and the chain grows. The first two, the leader and his assistant remain at the ends throughout the activity and are the only ones who can tag. When the chain surrounds a child, he may not break through the line or go under the hands. When the chain breaks, it must be reunited before tagging begins again. The game can end when the chain has five or more children. A new leader is chosen and the game begins again.

Suggested Application. In this game it is important for the children to keep a firm grasp on each other's hands, particularly as the chain grows. The children should discern the importance of this since the success of the activity depends upon it.

Hook On

One child is selected to be the runner. The remaining children form groups of four. The children in each of these groups of four stand one behind the other with arms around the waist of the child in front. The runner attempts to hook on at the end of any group of four where he can. The group members twist and swing about, trying to protect their end from being caught. If the runner is successful, the leader of that group is the new runner. The group having the most of its original members at the end of a specified period of time is the winner.

Suggested Application. The children need to exercise ingenuity as a group to protect the last person. Thus, the importance of being linked together as a group can be seen.

Rhythmic Activities

Most rhythmic activities involve tactile sensitivity, particularly those classified as movement songs and dances. In these kinds of activities the entire group, or partners, move in various patterns with hands joined. In addition, various forms of body contact are involved in swinging a partner, clapping hands with a partner and the like. Two examples of these kinds of activities follow.

Charlie Over the Water
Verse:

1. Charlie over the water.
2. Charlie over the sea.
3. Charlie caught a blackbird.
4. Can't catch me.

Action: One child is selected to be Charlie. The rest of the children form a circle and join hands. Charlie stands about two or three feet inside the circle. As the verse is sung, the children comprising the circle walk around counterclockwise while Charlie walks inside the circle clockwise. On the last word of the verse, all of the children stoop down. Charlie tries to tag the nearest child before he gets down. The activity continues with another child selected as Charlie.

Rabbit in the Hollow
Verse:

1. Rabbit in the hollow sits and sleeps.
2. Hunter in the forest nearer creeps.

3. Little rabbit, have a care.
4. Deep within your hollow there.
5. Quickly to the forest,
6. You must run, run, run.

Action: The children form a circle with hands joined. One child, taking the part of the rabbit, crouches inside the circle while another child, taking the part of the hunter, stands outside the circle. A space nearby is designated as the rabbit's home, to which he may run and in which he is safe. On lines 1 and 2 the children in the circle walk clockwise. On lines 3 and 4, the children in the circle stand still and the rabbit tries to get away from the hunter by breaking through the circle and attempting to reach home without being tagged. If the rabbit is tagged, he chooses another child to be the rabbit. The hunter chooses another hunter.

Stunt Activities

Stunt activities provide fine possibilities for tactility, in that many of them afford opportunities for body contact with other children as well as with the surface area. Some representative examples of these kinds of activities follow.

Seal Crawl. In the Seal Crawl the child supports himself on his hands while his body is extended back. The child squats and places his hands shoulder-width apart, palms flat and fingers pointed forward. He extends his legs in back of himself until his body is straight. The child points his toes to move forward on his hands, dragging his feet.

Churn the Butter. Churn the Butter involves two children. These two turn back-to-back and lock elbows by bending their arms to approximately a 90-degree angle. The elbows are held in back of each performer and the forearms are held against the ribs. One child picks up the other child from the surface area by bending forward with a slow, controlled movement. The other child will momentarily have his feet off the surface area. The first child releases the lifting force by straightening to an erect standing position; the other child then lifts the first child in the same manner. This action is repeated as long as desired. Children of nearly the same weight and strength should be paired for this stunt.

Wheelbarrow. Each child has a partner of about equal size and strength. One of the pair assumes a position with his hands on the surface area, his elbows straight, and his feet extended behind him. The other child carries the feet of the first child, who keeps his knees straight. He becomes a wheelbarrow by walking on his hands. Positions are changed so that each can become the wheelbarrow.

Tumbling Activities

Tumbling activities such as the Log Roll, Forward Roll, and Backward Roll (explained previously) are useful for tactile sensitivity. In addition to these, the following are of value for the same purpose.

Side Roll. The child assumes the starting position by kneeling on the mat and placing his forehead on it as near his knees as possible. He then grasps his shins with his hands and pulls his feet from the mat. The objective is for the child to start to roll to either side, roll to the back, to the other side, and back to the knees and forehead position. The child should concentrate on rolling in a straight pattern along the mat.

Egg Roll. In the Egg Roll the child should roll from a sitting position to his side, to his back to his other side, and back to the sitting position. The start is a sitting position on the mat with the knees close to the chest and the heels close to the buttocks. The child reaches inside his knees with his hands and grasps the outside of his shins. He is now ready to move to his side, in either direction, on his back, to his other side, and back to the sitting position.

VISUAL AND AUDITORY PERCEPTION

The visual and auditory systems provide two of the most important forms of sensory input for learning. The term *visual* is concerned with images that are obtained through the eyes. Thus, visual input involves the various learning media directed to the visual sense. The term *auditory* may be described as stimulation occurring through the sense organs of hearing. Therefore, auditory input is concerned with the various learning media directed to the auditory sense.

These two forms of sensory input complement each other in individuals who have both normal vision and hearing. However, as the extremes away from normalcy are approached—that is, in the case of complete or near-complete absence of one of the senses—their use as combined learning media obviously diminishes. However, at the extremes of normalcy, a person relies a great deal upon the system which is functioning normally. For example, although the sightless person relies a great deal upon tactile perception, particularly as far as "reading" is concerned, he is also extremely sensitive to auditory input in the form of various sounds. In a like manner, the deaf person relies heavily upon the visual sense as a form of sensory input.

The relationship of these two senses in children with normal or near-normal functioning of both is seen in the area of reading. That is, there is a natural sequence from listening to reading, and the acquisition of the skill of auditory discrimination is an important factor in learning to read. Additionally, in many teaching-learning situations these two forms of sensory input are used in combination; for example, the teacher might use oral communication to describe something and display it at the same time. Of course, one of the important features for teachers to consider is the extent to which these aspects of sensory input should be used simultaneously. The teacher needs to be aware of how well children can handle the tasks together. In other words, if visual and auditory input are combined in a teaching-learning situation, the teacher must determine whether or not, and to what extent, one becomes an attention-distracting factor for the other.

Visual Perception

Visual perception is the mental interpretation of what a person sees. A number of aspects of visual perception that have been identified include eye-motor coordination, figure-ground perception, form constancy, position in space, and spatial relationships. It has been suggested that children who show deficiency in these various areas may have difficulty in school performance. Various training programs have been devised to help correct or improve these conditions in children, with the idea that such training would result in the improvement of learning ability. The extent to which this has been accomplished has been extolled by some but seriously questioned by others. As indicated previously, research involving this general type of training does not present clear-cut and definitive evidence to support the notion that such training results in academic achievement. Perhaps it should be pointed out again that compensatory motor learning experiences do *not* provide for structured training in the attempt to bring about improvement in learning ability. This is to say that the activities provided in Part II of this book are those that are natural activities in the movement experiences of children. And, although there is a lack of objective evidence to support the idea that participation in such activities brings about absolute improvement in learning ability, there is nevertheless abundant observational support to justify children's participation in these activities.

Visual-Input Phase of Teaching

There are certain fundamental phases involved in almost every teaching-learning situation. These phases are (1) auditory input (to be discussed later in the chapter), (2) visual input, (3) participation, and (4) evaluation. Although some of these phases will be more important than others, they should occur in the teaching of practically every lesson regardless of the type of activity being taught. While the application of the phases may be general in nature, they nevertheless should be utilized in such a way that they become specific in a particular situation. Depending upon the type of activity being taught—game, rhythm, or self-testing activity—the use and application of the various phases should be characterized by flexibility and awareness of the objective of the lesson.

Various estimates indicate that the visual sense brings up upwards of three-fourths of our knowledge. If this postulation can be used as a valid criterion, the merits of the visual input phase in teaching are readily discernible.

In general, there are two types of visual input which can be used satisfactorily. These are visual symbols and human demonstration (live performance).

Visual Symbols

Included among the visual symbols are motion pictures and various kinds of flat or still pictures. One of the disadvantages of the latter centers around the difficulty of portraying movement with a still figure. Although movement is shown in motion pictures, it is not depicted in the third dimension which causes some degree of ineffectiveness. One valuable use of visual symbols is that which employs diagrams to show dimensions of playing areas. This procedure may be useful when the teaching is explaining an activity in the classroom before moving to the outdoor activity area. Court dimensions and the like can be diagrammed on the chalkboard, providing a good opportunity for integration with other areas such as mathematics and drawing to scale.

Human Demonstration

Some of the guides to action in the use of demonstration follow.

1. If the teacher plans to demonstrate, this should be included in preparation of the lesson by practicing and rehearsing the demonstration.
2. The teacher does not need to do all of the demonstrating; in fact, in some cases it may be much more effective to have one or more children demonstrate. Since the teacher is expected to be a skilled performer, a demonstration by a child will oftentimes serve to show other children that one of their own classmates can perform the activity and that they might also be able to do it. In addition, it may be entirely possible that the teacher may not be an efficient enough performer to demonstrate a certain activity. For example, it may be necessary for some teachers to call up children to demonstrate some of the more complex stunt and tumbling activities.
3. If the teacher prefers to do the demonstrating in a given situation, it still may be advisable to use children to demonstrate in order to show the class that the performance of the activity is within its realm of achievement.
4. The demonstration should be based upon the skill and ability of a given group of children. If it appears to be too difficult for them, they may not want to attempt the activity.
5. When at all possible, a demonstration should parallel the timing and conditions of the activity. However, if the situation is one in which the movements are complex or done with great speed, it might be a good idea to have the demonstration conducted at a slower pace than that involved in the actual playing or performance.
6. The group should be arranged so everyone is in a favorable position to see the demonstration. Moreover, the children should be able to view the demonstration from a position in which it takes place. For example, if the activity is to be performed in a lateral plane, children should be placed so that they can see it from this position.
7. Although demonstration and auditory input can be satisfactorily combined in many situations, as mentioned previously, care should be taken that an explanation is not lost because the visual sense offsets the auditory sense. That is, one sense should not become an attention-distracting factor for the other.
8. After the demonstration has been presented, it may be a good

practice to demonstrate again and to have the children go through the movements with the demonstrator. This allows the use of both the kinesthetic sense and the visual sense, closely integrating these two sensory stimuli.

9. Demonstrations should not be too long. Children are eager to participate, and this opportunity should be provided as soon as possible after the demonstration.

COMPENSATORY MOTOR LEARNING EXPERIENCES INVOLVING VISUAL PERCEPTION

The activities that follow are primarily concerned with *visualization* and *visual-motor coordination*. Visualization involves visual image, which is the mental construction of a visual experience, or the result of mentally combining a number of visual experiences. Visual-motor coordination is concerned with visual-motor tasks that involve the integration of vision and movement.

Jump the Shot

The children form a circle, with one child standing in the center holding a length of rope with an object tied to one end. The object should be something soft, such as a beanbag. The player in the center starts the game by swinging the object on the rope around and around close to the feet of the players in the circle. The players in the circle attempt to avoid being hit by the object by jumping over it when it goes by them. A point can be scored against any person hit on the feet by the object on the rope.

Suggested Application. This activity provides a good opportunity for visual-motor coordination, as a child must quickly coordinate his movement with the visual experience. This can be a good evaluation technique for the teacher, since it can be seen how well a child makes the judgments necessary to jump over the object at the proper time.

Ball Pass

The players are divided into two or more groups and each group forms a circle. The object of the game is to pass the ball around the circle to see who can get it around first. The teacher gives the directions for the ball to be passed or tossed from one player to another. For example, the teacher may say, "Pass the ball to the right," "Toss the ball over two players," and so on. The game may be varied by using more than one ball of different sizes and weights. For instance, a basketball, volleyball, and tennis ball might be used.

Suggested Application. This activity provides a good opportunity to improve eye-hand coordination, and it has been observed that after practice in this activity poor coordination can be improved.

Policeman

One child is selected to be the policeman, and sides are chosen. The groups stand equidistant from the policeman. The policeman carries a card, red on one side and green on the other. At the signal to go (green) from the policeman, each group sees how far it can get before the stop signal (red) is given. Any child who moves after the stop signal is given must go back to the original starting point. When all members of a side have passed the policeman, that group is declared the winner.

Suggested Application. Rather than using the colors, the words *Stop* and *Go* can be used so that the children can become familiar with the words as well as the colors. This activity helps children coordinate movement with visual experience. This game can help children become more adept at visual-motor association. The teacher should be alert to observe those children who do not stop on signal, as well as those who look to others for clues.

Keep It Up

Depending upon the ability level of the children, a large rubber playground ball, a beach ball, or even a large balloon can be used for this activity. Children are divided into several small circles, with each circle having a ball. On a signal, one child tosses the ball into the air and the other children try to see how long they can keep the ball up without letting it touch the surface area. The group that keeps it in the air for the longest time is the winner.

Suggested Application. This activity can be used for the improvement of eye-hand coordination.

Figure Relay

Two lines are drawn about 30 feet apart on the activity area. The group is divided into two teams. Both teams stand behind one of the lines. The teacher displays the form of a geometric figure cut out of cardboard. The teams run across to the opposite line and form the figure. The team that forms the figure correctly first wins a point. The teams then line up behind that line, and when the teacher displays another figure, they run to the opposite line and again form the figure the teacher has displayed. The geometric figures should be those that the children have been working with such as the circle, square, rectangle, and triangle.

Suggested Application. This activity can be useful in improving form perception. It helps children work together to produce a given form that is displayed by the teacher. It has been observed that children who have problems with figure-ground relationships may also have difficulty with form perception. Thus, this activity can be of value to those children who have problems in both figure-ground relationships and form perception.

Mother May I (variation)

The children stand in a line at one end of the activity area. The teacher has cards showing object pairs, similar and different. The teacher holds up one pair of the cards. If the paired objects or symbols are the same, the children may take one giant step forward. Any child who moves when he sees an unpaired set of cards must return to the starting line. The object of the game is to reach the finish line on the opposite side of the activity area.

Suggested Application. The teacher may select cards to test any level of visual discrimination. Using pairs of cards for categorizing pictures would utilize concept and language development.

Rhythmic Activities

Many of the movement songs and dances can provide opportunities for training in figure-ground relationships and improvement in form perception. In addition to the development of forms in certain dance patterns, the different formations for dances such as line, circle, and square are useful experiences for children.

Numerous dances provide for eye-hand and eye-foot coordination and, as such, are valuable experiences in developing those forms of visual perception. A specific example is *Children's Polka* described previously.

Ball-Handling Activities

The various kinds of ball-handling activities provide outstanding experiences for eye-hand coordination. Many of these activities have been described previously.

Balance Beam Activities

Activities on the balance beam provide many good opportunities for the development of a child's ability to discern figure-ground relationships. Many of these activities have been described previously.

Auditory Perception

It was estimated several years ago that about 75 percent of the waking hours is spent in verbal communication—45 percent in listening, 30 percent in speaking, 16 percent in reading and the remaining 9 percent in writing. If this estimate can be used as a valid criterion, the importance of developing listening skills cannot be denied. If children are going to learn to listen effectively, care should be taken to improve upon their auditory perception—the mental interpretation of what a person hears.

Auditory-Input Phase of Teaching

Before getting into some of the specific activities involving auditory perception, it seems appropriate to discuss certain factors concerned with the auditory-input phase of teaching. In this regard, the factors taken into account here are (1) preparing the children for listening, (2) teacher-child and child-child interaction, and (3) directionality of sound.

Preparing the Children for Listening

Since it is likely that the initial part of the auditory-input phase will originate with the teacher, care should be taken to prepare the children for listening. The teacher may set the scene by relating the activity to the interests of the children. In addition, the teacher should be on the alert to help children develop their own reasons for listening.

In preparing children to listen, the teacher should be aware that it is of extreme importance to take into consideration the comfort of the children, and that attempts should be made to alleviate any possible distractions. Although evidence concerning the effect of environmental distractions on listening effectiveness is in short supply, there is reason to believe that distraction does interfere with listening comprehension. Moreover, being able to see, as well as hear the speaker, is an important factor in listening comprehension.

All of these factors have a variety of implications for the auditory-input phase of the teaching-learning situation. For example, consideration should be given to the placement of children when an activity is being explained to them. This means, for instance, that if the teacher is providing auditory input from a circle formation, he or she should be a part of the circle instead of speaking from the center of the circle. Moreover, if the group is large, perhaps it would be best to place the children in a small group for the auditory-input phase and then put them into formation for the activity. Also, it might be wise for teachers to consider that an object, such as a ball, could become an attention-distracting factor when an activity is being explained. The attention of the children is sometimes focused on the ball and they may not listen to what is being said. The teacher might wish to conceal such an object until time for its use is most appropriate.

Teacher-Child and Child-Child Interaction

Since the auditory-input phase is a two-way process, it is important to take into account certain factors involving verbal interaction of children with children and children with the teacher.

By "democracy" some people seem to mean everyone doing or saying whatever happens to cross his mind at the moment, and this raises the question of control. It is to be emphasized that *group discussions,* if they are to be democratic and if they are to be productive, must be under control. In brief, disciplined, controlled group discussion can be good training for living in a society in which both individual and group interests are profoundly respected.

Another important function in teacher-child verbal interaction is that concerned with time given to questions after the teacher has given an explanation. The teacher should give time for questions from the group but should be very skillful in the use of questions. It must be determined immediately whether or not a question is a legitimate one. This implies that the type of question asked can help to serve as criteria for the teacher to evaluate the auditory-input phase of teaching. For example, if numerous questions are asked, it is apparent that either the auditory input from the teacher was incomplete or the children were not paying attention.

Directionality of Sound

In summarizing recent findings concerned with directionality of sound there are a number of interesting factors which are important to the auditory-input phase. Individuals tend to initiate movement toward the direction from which the sound cue emanates. For example, if a given verbal cue instructs an individual to move a body segment or segments to the left but emanates from the right side of the individual, the initial motor response is to the right, followed by a reverse response to the left. Emphasizing the importance of this for children, it is recommended that when working on direction of motor responses, one should make certain that sound cues come from the direction in which the motor response is to be made. The point to stress is that children have enough difficulty in discriminating left from right without further confounding them.

COMPENSATORY MOTOR LEARNING EXPERIENCES INVOLVING AUDITORY PERCEPTION

Stoop Tag

The children form a circle and join hands. One child is *It* and stands in the center of the circle. The children walk around the circle saying,

I am happy! I am free!
I am down! You can't catch me!

At the word "down," the children stoop and let go of each other's hands. Then they stand up and jump and hop about, daring the child who is *It* to tag them. They must stoop to avoid being tagged. If a child is tagged when he is not stooping, he becomes *It*.

Suggested Application. The child first learns to act on the basis of verbal instructions by others. In this regard it has been suggested that later he learns to guide and direct his own behavior on the basis of his own language activities—he literally talks to himself, giving himself instructions. This point of view has been supported by research which postulates that speech is a form of communication between children and adults that later becomes a means of organizing the child's own behavior. That is, the function which was previously divided between two people—

child and adult—later becomes a function of human behavior. The point in this activity is that the child tells himself what to do and then does it. He says, "I am down" and then carries out this action.

Dog Chase

The class is divided into five or six groups. The members of each group are given the name of a dog, such as collie, poodle, and so on. The small groups then mingle into one large group. One child, acting as the leader, throws a ball or other object away from the groups, at the same time calling out one of the dog names. All of the children with this dog name run after the object. The one who gets possession of it first becomes the leader for the next time.

Suggested Application. The teacher can use this activity as a diagnostic technique by observing those children who react slowly or do not react at all to the auditory input.

Mouse and Cheese

A round mousetrap is formed by the children standing in a circle. In the center of the mousetrap is placed the cheese (a ball or some other object). The children are then assigned consonant digraphs *sh, ch, th.* Several of the children will have the same consonant digraph. That is, if there are 30 children, three will have the same consonant digraph. When the teacher calls a word beginning with a consonant digraph, all the children with this digraph run around the circle and back to their original place, representing a hole in the trap. Through these original places they run into the circle to get the cheese. The child who gets the cheese is the winning mouse. Another word is called and the same procedure is followed. Children may be assigned different digraphs from time to time.

Suggested Application. Children need repetition in order to develop the ability to hear and identify various sound elements within words. This game enables children to recognize consonant digraphs within the context of whole words. A variation of this game would be to focus on ending consonant digraphs.

Stunt Activities

One of the ways of providing for auditory-motor association is stunt activities. For example, young children like to perform animal imitations.

When they learn how to perform the various stunts, the teacher can identify the stunts by name and have them change from one stunt to another by calling out the name of the stunt. Two examples of such animal imitations follow.

Puppy Dog Run

The child places his hands, palms flat and fingers forward, on the surface area in front of his feet. The hands should be under the shoulders for support. The child bends his legs slightly to allow his back to move parallel with the surface area. He then walks forward using both arms and both legs to mimic a running dog. The gait can be increased as the child becomes more proficient.

Elephant Walk

From an erect standing position, the child bends forward at the waist until his back is parallel with the surface area. His arms are straight and held beneath his shoulders. His legs remain straight throughout the walk. As the child steps slowly, he swings his arms from side to side. The swaying motion will resemble an elephant swinging the trunk as it walks.

All of the contemporary motor learning experiences presented in Part II of the book have been used with success in improving learning ability when applied in the appropriate manner.

PART III
COGNITIVE MOTOR LEARNING

Chapter 8

OVERVIEW

In the Introduction to the book I identified cognitive motor learning as that branch of motor learning which is essentially concerned with academic skill and concept development. This means that children can be helped to develop these skills and concepts while actively engaged in certain motor learning experiences.

Although all children differ in one or more characteristics, the fact remains that they are more *alike* than they are different. The one common likeness of all children is that they all *move*. Cognitive motor learning is based essentially on the theory that children will learn better when what I will call *academic learning* takes place through pleasurable physical activity. That is, when the *motor* component operates at a maximal level in skill and concept development in school subject areas essentially oriented to *verbal* learning. This is not to say that *motor* and *verbal* learning are two mutually exclusive kinds of learning, although it has been suggested that at the two extremes the dichotomy appears justifiable. It is recognized that in verbal learning, which involves almost complete abstract symbolic manipulations, there may be, among others, such motor components as tension, subvocal speech, and physiological changes in metabolism which operate at a minimal level. It is also recognized that in motor activity where the learning is predominantly motor in nature, verbal learning is evident, although perhaps at a minimal level. For example, in teaching an activity involving motor learning, there is a certain amount of verbalization (talking) in developing a kinesthetic concept of the particular activity that is being taught.

The procedure of cognitive motor learning involves the selection of an activity such as an active game, rhythmic activity, or self-testing activity which is taught to the children and used as a learning medium for the development of a skill or concept in a specific subject area. An attempt is made to arrange an active learning situation so that a fundamental intellectual skill or concept if practiced or rehearsed in the course of participating in the motor learning experience.

Essentially, there are two general types of such activities. One type is useful for developing a specific concept where the learner *acts out* the concept and thus is able to visualize as well as to get the *feel* of the concept. Concepts become a part of the child's physical reality, so to speak, as the child participates in the activity where the concept is inherent. An example of such an activity follows.

The concept to be developed is the science concept *electricity travels along a pathway and needs a complete circuit over which to travel.* A motor learning activity in which this concept is inherent is *Straddle Ball Roll.*

The children stand one behind the other in relay files with six to ten children in each file. All are in stride position with feet far enough apart so that a ball can be rolled between the legs of the players. The first person in each file holds a rubber playground ball. At a signal the person in front of each file starts the activity by attempting to roll the ball between the legs of all the players on his team. The team that gets the ball to the last member first in the manner described scores a point. The last player goes to the head of the file, and this procedure is continued with a point scored each time for the team that gets the ball back to the last player first. After every player has had an opportunity to roll the ball back the team that has scored the most points is declared the winner.

In applying this activity to develop the concept the first player at the head of each file becomes the electric switch which opens and shuts the current. The ball is the electric current. As the ball rolls between the children's legs it moves right through if all of the legs are properly lined up. When a leg is not in the proper stride, the path of the ball is impeded and the ball rolls out. The activity has to be stopped until the ball is recovered and the correction made in the position of the leg. The circuit has to be repaired (the child's leg) before the flow of electricity (roll of the ball) can be resumed.

The second type of motor learning activity helps to develop skills by using these skills in a highly interesting and stimulating situations. Repetitive practice for the development of skills related to specific concepts can be utilized. An example of this type of motor learning activity follows.

This activity is an adaptation of the game *Steal the Bacon* and is used for the practice of *initial consonants.* Children are put into two groups of seven each. The members of both teams are given the letters *b, c, d, h, m, n,* and *p* or any other initial consonants with which they have been having difficulty. The teams face each other about 10 feet apart as in the following diagram.

b		p
c		n
d		m
h	beanbag	h
	(bacon)	
m		d
n		c
p		b

The teacher calls out a word such as *ball,* and the two children having the letter *b* run out to grab the beanbag. If a player gets the beanbag back to his line, he scores two points for his team. If his opponent tags him before he gets back, the other team scores one point. The game ends when each letter has been called. The scores are totalled and the game is repeated with the children being identified with different letters.

HOW COGNITIVE MOTOR LEARNING FACILITATES CHILD LEARNING

During the early school years, and at ages six to eight particularly, it is likely that learning is limited frequently by a relatively short attention span rather than only by intellectual capabilities. Moreover, some children who do not appear to think or learn well in abstract terms can more readily grasp concepts when given an opportunity to use them in an applied manner. In view of the fact that the child is a creature of movement, and also that he is likely to deal better in concrete rather than abstract terms, it would seem to follow naturally that the cognitive motor learning medium is well-suited for him.

The above statement should not be interpreted to mean that I am suggesting that learning through movement-oriented experiences (motor learning) and passive learning experiences (verbal learning) are two different kinds of learning. The position is taken here that *learning is learning,* even though in the cognitive motor learning approach the motor component may be operating at a higher level than in most of the traditional types of learning activities.

The theory of learning accepted here is that learning takes place in terms of reorganization of the systems of perception into a functional and integrated whole because of the result of certain stimuli. This implies that problem solving is a way of desirable and worthwhile human learning and that learning can take place well through problem solving. In a cognitive motor learning situation that is well planned, a great deal of consideration should be given to the inherent possibilities for learning in terms of problem solving. In this approach opportunities abound for near-ideal teaching-learning situations because of the many problems to be solved. Using active games as an example, the following sample questions asked by children indicate that there is a great opportunity for reflective thinking, use of judgment, and problem solving in this type of experience.

1. Why didn't I get to touch the ball more often?
2. How can we make it a better game?
3. Would two circles be better than one?
4. How can I learn to throw the ball better?

Another very important factor to consider with respect to the cognitive motor learning medium is that a considerable part of the learnings of young children are motor in character, with the child devoting a good proportion of his attention to skills of a locomotor nature. Furthermore, learnings of a motor nature tend to usurp a large amount of the young child's time and energy, and are often closely associated with other learnings. In addition, it is well known by experienced classroom teachers at the primary level that the child's motor mechanism is active to the extent that it is almost an impossibility for him to remain for a very long period of time in a quiet state regardless of the passiveness of the learning situation.

To demand prolonged sedentary states of children is actually, in a sense, in defiance of a basic physiological principle. This is concerned directly with the child's basal metabolism. The term *metabolism* is concerned with physical and chemical changes in the body which involve producing and consuming energy. The rate at which the physical and chemical processes are carried on when the individual is in a state of rest represents his *basal metabolism*. Thus, the basal metabolic rate is indicative of the speed at which body fuel is changed to energy as well as how fast this energy is used.

Basal metabolic rate can be measured in terms of calories per meter of body surface, with a calorie representing a unit measure of heat energy in food. It has been found that, on the average, basal metabolism rises from birth to about two or three years of age, at which time it starts to decline until the ages of 20 to 24. Also, the rate is higher for boys than for girls. With the high metabolic rate, and therefore the greatest amount of energy occurring during the early school years, deep consideration might well be given to learning activities through which this energy can be utilized. Moreover it has been observed that there is an increased attention span during participation in motor learning activities. When a task such as a motor learning activity is meaningful to a child, he can spend longer periods engaged in it than is likely to be the case in some of the more traditional types of learning activities.

The comments made thus far have alluded to some of the *general* aspects of the value of cognitive motor learning. The ensuing discussions will focus more specifically on what might arbitrarily be called *inherent facilitative factors* in the cognitive motor learning medium which are highly compatible with child learning. These factors are *motivation, proprioception,* and *reinforcement,* all of which are somewhat interdependent and interrelated.

Motivation

In consideration of motivation as an inherent facilitative factor in cognitive motor learning, the term could be thought of as it is described in the *Dictionary of Education;* that is, "the practical art of applying incentives and arousing interest for the purpose of causing a pupil to perform in a desired way."

One should also take into account *extrinsic* and *intrinsic* motivation. Extrinsic motivation is described as "the application of incentives that are external to a given activity to make work palatable and to facilitate performance," while intrinsic motivation is the "determination of behavior that is resident within an activity and that sustains it, as with autonomous acts and interests."

Extrinsic motivation has been and continues to be used as a means of spurring individuals to achievement. This most often takes the form of various kinds of reward incentives. The main objection to this type of motivation is that it may tend to focus the learner's attention upon the reward rather than the learning task and the total learning situation.

In general, the child is motivated when he discovers what seems to him to be a suitable reason for engaging in a certain activity. The most valid reason, of course, is that he sees a purpose for the activity and derives enjoyment from it. The child must feel that what he is doing is important and purposeful. When this occurs and the child gets the impression that he is being successful in a group situation, the motivation is intrinsic; it comes about naturally as a result of the child's interest in the activity. It is the premise here that cognitive motor learning in the form of active games, rhythmic activities, and self-testing activities contain this *built in* ingredient so necessary to desirable and worthwhile learning.

The ensuing discussions of this section of the chapter will be concerned with two aspects of motivation that are considered to be inherent in cognitive motor learning: (1) motivation in relation to *interest*, and (2) motivation in relation to *knowledge of results*.

Motivation in Relation to Interest

It is important to have an understanding of the meaning of interest as well as an appreciation of how interests function as an adjunct to learning. As far as the meaning of the term is concerned, *interest* could be considered as a state of being, a way of reacting to a certain situation. *Interests* can be thought of as those fields or areas to which a child reacts with interest consistently over an extended period of time.

A good condition for learning is a situation in which a child agrees with and acts upon the learnings that he considers of most value to him. This means that the child accepts as most valuable those things that are of greatest interest to him. To the very large majority of children physical activity experiences are likely to be of the greatest personal value.

Under most circumstances a very high interest level is concomitant with pleasurable physical activities simply because of the expectation of pleasure children tend to associate with such activities. The structure of a learning activity is directly related to the length of time the learning act can be tolerated by the learner without loss of interest. Motor learning experiences by their very nature are more likely to be so structured than many of the traditional learning activities.

Motivation in Relation to Knowledge of Results

Knowledge of results is most commonly referred to as *feedback* which is the process of providing the learner with information as to how accurate his reactions were. Or, knowledge of various kinds which the performer received about his performance.

Many learning theorists feel that knowledge of results is the strongest, most important variable controlling performance and learning, and further, that studies have repeatedly shown that there is no improvement without it, progressive improvement with it, and deterioration after its withdrawal. As a matter of fact, there appears to be sufficient objective evidence to indicate that learning is usually more effective when one receives some immediate information on how he is progressing. It would appear rather obvious that such knowledge of results is an important adjunct to learning because one would have little idea of which of his responses were correct. Some learning theorists make the analogy that it would be like trying to learn a task while blindedfolded.

The cognitive motor learning medium provides almost instantaneous knowledge of results because the child can actually *see* and *feel* himself throw a ball, or tag or be tagged in a game. He does not become the victim of a poorly constructed paper-and-paper test, the results of which may have little or no meaning for him.

Proprioception

It was stated earlier that the theory of learning accepted here is that learning takes place in terms of a reorganization of the systems of perception into a functional and integrated whole as a result of certain stimuli. These systems of perception, or sensory processes as they are sometimes referred to, are ordinarily considered to consist of the senses of sight, hearing, touch, smell, and taste. Although this point of view is convenient for some purposes, it greatly oversimplifies the ways by which information can be fed into the human organism. A number of sources of sensory input are overlooked, particularly the senses that enable the body to maintain its correct posture. As a matter of fact, the 60 or 70 pounds of muscle which include over 600 in number that are attached to the skeleton of the averaged-sized man could well be his most important sense organs.

Various estimates indicate that the visual sense brings us more than three-fourths of our knowledge. Therefore, it could be said with little reservation that man is *eye-minded.* However, one of my former contemporaries, the late Dr. Arthur Steinhaus, a notable physiologist, once reported that a larger portion of the nervous system is devoted to receiving and integrating sensory input originating in the muscles and joint structures than is devoted to the eye and ear combined. In view of this it could be contended that man is also *muscle sense*-minded.

Generally speaking, *proprioception* is concerned with muscle sense.

The proprioceptors are sensory nerve terminals that give information concerning movements and position of the body. A proprioceptive feedback mechanism is involved which, in a sense, regulates movement. In view of the fact that children are so movement-oriented, it appears a reasonable speculation that proprioceptive feedback from the receptors of the muscles, skin, and joints may contribute in a facilitative manner when the cognitive motor learning medium is used to develop academic skills and concepts. The combination of the psychological factor of motivation and the physiological factor of proprioception inherent in the cognitive motor learning medium has caused me to coin the term motor vation to describe this phenomenon.

One writer once characterized my concept of this in the following manner.

> Humphrey presents highly persuasive evidence for the effectiveness of his concepts. He suggests that sensory experiences arising from muscle action acts as a kind of coordinating process that aids in the integration of visual and auditory input, forming a holistic kind of perceptual experience as a child moves his body and limbs in the activities he had devised.[1]

Reinforcement

In considering the compatibility of cognitive motor learning with reinforcement theory, the meaning of reinforcement needs to be taken into account. An acceptable general description of reinforcement is that there is an increase in the efficiency of a response to a stimulus brought about by the concurrent action of another stimulus. A simple example of this would be when a teacher gives praise and encouragement when a child is engaged in a task. Generally, the same principle applies when athletes refer to the "home court advantage." That is, the home fans are present to spur them on. The basis for contending that cognitive motor learning is consistent with general reinforcement theory is that it reinforces attention to the learning task and learning behavior. It keeps the child involved in the learning activity, which is perhaps the major area of application for reinforcement procedures. Moreover, there is perhaps little in the way of human behavior that is not reinforced, or at least reinforcible, by feedback of some sort. The importance of proprioceptive feedback has already been discussed in this particular connection.

---

[1]Cratty, Bryant J., *Physical Expressions of Intelligence*, Englewood Cliffs, New Jersey, Prentice-Hall, 1972, p. 49.

In summarizing this discussion, it would appear that cognitive motor learning establishes a more effective situation for learning reinforcement for the following reasons.

1. The greater motivation of the children in the cognitive motor learning situation involves emphasis on those behaviors directly pertinent to their learning activities, making these salient for the purpose of reinforcement.
2. The proprioceptive emphasis in cognitive motor learning involves a greater number of *responses* associated with and conditioned to learning stimuli.
3. The gratifying aspects of cognitive motor learning provide a generalized situation of *reinforcers*.

EVIDENCE TO SUPPORT THE THEORY

Any approach to learning should be based, at least to some degree, upon objective evidence produced by experimental research, and this is the subject of the following discussion.

There are a number of acceptable ways of studying how behavioral changes take place in children. In this regard, over a period of years I have conducted numerous controlled studies concerned with the cognitive motor learning approach. The findings are suggestive enough to give rise to some interesting conclusions, which may be briefly summarized as follows.

1. In general, children tend to learn certain academic skills and concepts better through the cognitive motor learning medium than through many of the traditional approaches.
2. This approach, while favorable to both boys and girls, appears to be more favorable for boys.
3. This approach appears to be more favorable for children with average and below average intelligence.
4. For children with higher levels of intelligence, it may be possible to introduce more advanced concepts at an earlier age through this approach.

In addition to the above scientific findings, the many successful experiences with cognitive motor learning recommended through this book should encourage teachers and others to use the approach in an effort to help children learn by means of pleasurable and enjoyable experiences.

Cognitive motor learning as conceived here has come to be designated as the "Humphrey Program of Child Learning Through Motor Activity," and it has received rather widespread recognition.

Statement abstracts about it have been distributed to scholars in 55 countries. The Center for the Study of World Psychologies has distributed some of my research studies about the Program to interested individual and research groups in Russia and Japan. And, the Program has been featured in a Voice of America broadcast and distributed to its 35 language centers.

Chapter 9

READING AND MOTOR LEARNING

It has been suggested that the ability to read was not considered important for most laymen until sometime after Johann Gutenberg invented the printing press in the fifteenth century, and the Protestant Reformation with its emphasis on individual interpretation of the Bible. Until that time, reading was generally restricted to the clergy and certain members of the nobility.[1]

Almost three centuries ago Francois Fénelon, the famous French educator and ecclesiastic, is reputed to have suggested that he had seen certain children who had learned to read while playing. Although I am not exactly sure what he meant, I am willing to rationalize that his statement might have been the first indication that there is a high degree of compatibility between reading and cognitive motor learning, and a forerunner of some of the thoughts and ideas expounded in this chapter.

DIMENSIONS OF THE READING ACT

In considering the role of motor learning in relation to children learning to read it is essential to consider what reading is, what its dimensions are, and then to examine motor components of the reading process. Any attempt to describe or to define the reading process is an awesome task if the attempt is to be a serious one. Such a task quickly reveals the complex nature of the reading process with its concomitant difficulties in identifying specific factors affecting success or lack of success in the reading act for each individual child.

The need to define or explain the reading process, however, is essential. It is well recognized that instructional procedures in reading are based on the teacher's concept of what reading is and how children learn to read.

Practically all of us learn to read, but, of course, with varying degrees

---

[1]The New Columbia Encyclopedia, New York, Columbia University Press, 4th ed., 1975, p. 2284.

of proficiency. Yet, to define exactly what reading means is not an easy task. A part of the reason for this is that it means different things to different people. It has been suggested that the psychologist thinks of reading as a thought process. Those who deal in semantics, which is the study of meanings, think of reading as the graphic representation of speech. The linguist, one who specializes in speech and language, is concerned with the sounds of language and its written form. Finally, the sociologist is concerned with the interaction of reading and culture.

As will be seen later in the chapter, reading is an aspect of communication. As such, reading becomes more than just being able to recognize a word on a printed page. To communicate, a meaning must be shared and the reader must be able to comprehend. Thus, one of the most important concerns in teaching reading is that of helping children develop comprehension skills.

Reading could be thought of as bringing meaning to the printed page instead of only gaining meaning *from* it. This means that the author of a reading selection does not necessarily convey ideas to the reader but stimulates him to construct them out of his own experience. (This is one of the major purposes of cognitive motor learning reading content which is dealt with later in the chapter.)

Since reading is such a complex act and it cannot be easily defined, I will resort to a rather broad and comprehensive description of the term. This description of reading is *an interpretation of written or printed verbal symbols.* This can range from graffiti on restroom walls to the Harvard Classics.

It should be borne in mind that the entire child reads; he reads with his senses, his experiences, his cultural heritage, and, of course, with his muscles. It is the latter aspect with which I am predominantly concerned in this chapter, because the aspect of "muscle sense" involved in cognitive motor learning is an extremely important dimension in reading for children.

MOTOR COMPONENTS OF READING

There are a number of motor components in the reading process. Two of these will be discussed here: the eye movements of the visual process itself and the sensorimotor aspects of perception and cognition.

Eye Movements in Reading

Early studies in reading focused on the visual act of reading as a means of better understanding of the process. Extensive research in this area continued through the 1940s. Such research resulted in the development of reading-eye cameras such as the Ophthalmograph (American Optical Company) by which eye movements could be recorded and analyzed.

From these studies the pattern of eye movements in the reading act is one of the eyes moving from left to right across the line of print with a return sweep to the next line, proceeding in a left-to-right direction again. This rhythmic movement line after line is broken by fixations as the eyes move across the line and regressions or backward movements.

At fixation points the eyes are not in motion. It is at this moment, however, that the vision is not blurred by movement and the visual act of reading takes place. The time of "fixation" may vary from a third to a fourth of a second and is affected by the skill development of the reader and the difficulty of the material. Approximately 90 percent of the time spent in reading is accounted for by fixation points when the reader is going through the "seeing," the word-recognition, and the association process.

Regressions occur when there is a breakdown in the word-recognition and association aspects of the reading process. The reader may regress along the same line or several lines in order to arrive at word recognition or comprehension of the idea being presented. Some reading specialists caution that an excessive proportion of unknown words, inadequate experiences with the multiple meanings of words, and reading matter which is much too complex for the child's experiences all promote a faulty reading pattern and lack of progress in reading.

Eye span is another term used in describing the visual act. Eye span is the span of recognition during the moment of "fixation." For the elementary school child the eye span may be limited to the point where there is an average of two fixation points per word. The limitations of the eye span also indicates the demand upon the eyes in terms of the number of times the eyes converge in perfect alignment to focus on each "fixation."

As a visual task, adequate vision for reading calls for coordination and motility with accurate binocular shifts from point to point, accurate focus and accomodation to distance, a fine degree of parallel or coordinated action of both eyes and left-to-right directional attack.

When there is difficulty of function in eye movements this can result in loss of place, omissions, excessive repetitions, and slow rate. Defects in coordination, motility, directional attack, and form perception can prevent development of a desirable pattern of eye movement.

When there is evidence of deficiencies in visual perception or eye-hand coordination, developmental training can be given. Three major types of visual training for perception and discrimination are: (1) directionality, or orientation to direction, (2) ocular motility, or promoting coordinated movements of both eyes, and (3) form perception, or discrimination of similarities and differences in designs, figures, and wordlike forms. (Some examples of how this training can be accomplished were presented in Part II of the book.)

The Sensorimotor Aspects of Perception and Cognition in Reading

Perception in the reading act is a functional sequence involving the stimulus of the printed words, the process of recognizing the word, and assigning meaning to it based on the reader's previous past experiences. At this point reading must also be considered a symbolic function in that it allows the reader to cognize through representational thought.

It could be argued that reading instruction oftentimes becomes inconsistent with what is declared essential in the reading process or what is recommended for the learning-to-read environment of children. With the ever-increasing emphasis on the higher-level cognitive processing in the reading experience there seems to be an inordinate focus on words in the abstract context rather than in the reality context.

Language growth is described within the total context of child development. As the child moves to the readiness stage for reading, his physical growth and environment are described as characteristically physically-oriented activities not as an end in themselves but as a means of manipulating the environment for other purposes. Such activities gradually include those involving finer muscle coordination. During this period there is also the characteristically tremendous energy which manifests itself in physical activity as mentioned previously in relation to basal metabolic rate. Interesting enough, over three decades ago David Russell related these characteristics of children's physical and mental growth to the organization of the reading program by stating:

The application of this physical development to the primary reading program are rather direct. Children in the first grade should engage in many physical activities and thus need a program involving something more than just sitting.[2]

It is interesting to note that his concept of the use of physically-oriented activities was limited to pacing and spacing with reading-oriented activities rather than using motor learning as a means of developing reading skills.

Recognition has been given to the need for training in visual perception skills. The sensorimotor aspects of the real experience, the bringing of physical reality to the printed word and page through proprioception are cited as facilitating and enhancing perception and cognition. The naturalness of the physically-oriented activity for beginning and early readers is recognized.

I am fully aware that the reading act ultimately emphasizes the representational nature of word symbols, and that the higher levels of cognition are abstract. But it is not an either-or situation. There is general agreement that the physical reality of concrete experiences aids comprehension. There is evidence that there is need for increased emphasis upon the use of physical reality of the child in his learning-to-read efforts. In the discussions later in the chapter I will present several activities utilizing motor learning that have been developed and found effective in skills development and establishing interest in and positive attitudes toward reading.

READING READINESS

There are certain *developmental tasks* that are important for children to accomplish. Reading can be considered as such a developmental task. That is, it is a task that a child needs to perform to satisfy his personal needs as well as those requirements which society and the culture impose upon him. In viewing reading as a developmental task, we can then consider reading readiness as a developmental *stage* at which certain factors have prepared the child for reading.

At one time, reading readiness was considered only as being concerned with the child being ready to *begin* the reading experience. In more recent years it has come to be thought of more in terms of each step of reading as one concerned with readiness for further reading. There-

---

[2]Russell, David, *Children Learn to Read,* New York, Ginn and Company, 1961, p. 81.

fore the idea of reading readiness is not confined only to the start of reading instruction but to the teaching and learning of most all reading skills. A given child may be considered ready to *learn to read* at a certain age. However, this same child may not necessarily be ready to *read to learn* until a later time. In fact, some reading specialists consider the primary level of grades one through three as a time for learning to read, and the intermediate level of grades four through six as a time when the child begins to read to learn.

Reading readiness needs to be thought of as a complex combination of basic abilities and conditions and not only as a single characteristic. This combination includes (1) various aspects of visual ability, (2) certain factors concerned with the auditory sense, (3) sex differences, (4) age, and (5) socioeconomic conditions. Obviously, it is not the purpose here to go into detail with reference to these various characteristics but merely to identify them at this point. Later in the chapter some specific recommendations will be made concerning the application and function of motor learning as a medium for dealing with certain aspects of reading readiness.

SCHOOL READING PROGRAMS

One of the very important school curriculum areas in childhood education is the *language arts* program. This program includes listening, speaking, reading, and writing, all of which are concerned with communication. The primary purpose of the language arts program in the modern elementary school is to facilitate communication.

Speaking and writing can be referred to as the *expressive* phases of language, while listening and reading are considered the *receptive* phases. This implies that through speaking and writing the individual has the opportunity to express his or her thoughts and feelings to others. Through reading and listening the individual receives the thoughts and feelings of others.

Although it has been indicated that the language arts program contains listening, speaking, reading, and writing, the reader should not interpret this to mean that these are considered as entirely separate entities. On the contrary, they are closely interrelated, and each can be considered a component part of the broad area of communication. Such areas of study as spelling, word meanings, and word recognition are involved in each of the four areas.

The importance of the interrelationship of the various language arts can be shown in different ways. For example, children must use words in speaking and have them meaningful before they can read them successfully. Also, they can spell better the words that they read with understanding and that they want to use for their own purposes. In addition, their handwriting even improves when they use it in purposeful and meaningful communication when someone they like is going to read it. Perhaps the two most closely interrelated and interdependent phases of the language arts are listening and reading. In fact, most reading specialists agree that learning to listen is the first step in learning to read. This relationship will be very apparent later in the chapter in the discussion of motor learning reading content.

The modern elementary school gives a great deal of attention to the interrelationship of the various phases of the language arts. This is reflected in the way in which language experiences are being provided for children in the better-than-average elementary school. In the traditional elementary school it was a common practice to treat such aspects of the language arts as reading, writing, and spelling as separate subjects. As a result, they became more or less isolated and unrelated entities, and their full potential as media of expression probably was never fully realized. In the more modern elementary school, where children have more freedom of expression and, consequently, great opportunity for self-expression, the approach to teaching languages arts is one that relates the various language areas to particular areas of interest. All of the phases of language arts—listening, speaking, reading, and writing—are thus used in the solution of problems in all curriculum areas. This procedure is primarily based upon the assumption that skill in communication should be developed in all of the activities engaged in by children.

It has already been stated that through reading the individual receives the thoughts and feelings of others; therefore, reading is considered a receptive phase of language. In this case the word *receptive* might well carry a figurative as well as purely literal meaning. Indeed, reading has been on the "receiving end" of a great deal of criticism over the years. Perhaps more criticism has been directed at it than all the other school subjects combined. Although it may be difficult to determine precisely why reading has suffered the brunt of attack, one could speculate that it might be because, in general, most people consider reading as the real test of learning. In fact, in the early days of American education, grade levels tended to be thought of as "readers": a child was said to be in the "first reader," "second reader," and so on.

A good bit of the controversy involving reading seems to center around two general areas. First, there has been criticism of the various methods of teaching reading, and second, there has been some question regarding the validity of the principles upon which these methods are based. Perhaps because of individual differences, any method used in absolute form to the exclusion of all other methods would not meet the needs of all children. For this reason it seems logical to assume that the procedures or combination of procedures employed should be those which best meet the needs of an individual child or a particular group of children.

It is not my purpose to extol or criticize any of the past or present methods of teaching reading. Rather, the content of this chapter is intended to show how cognitive motor learning experiences can be used to assist the child in his or her efforts to read.

DIAGNOSIS THROUGH MOTOR LEARNING

A standard general description of the term *diagnosis* is the act of identifying a condition from its signs and symptoms. Applied to reading, diagnosis implies an analysis of reading behavior for purposes of discovering strength and weaknesses of a child as a basis for more effective guidance of his reading efforts.

Among other things, it is important to try to discover why a child reads as he does, what he is able to read, and what he reads successfully. In addition, we need to know if he is having problems in reading, what these problems are, and the causes of the problems.

Many diagnostic tests are available for use, and they have various degrees of validity. Studies tend to show that teachers themselves can forecast reading success of first grade children with about as much accuracy as reading readiness tests. It may be that such success in teacher observation has been a part of the reason for what is called *diagnostic teaching* becoming today's byword as school systems address their attention to meeting the needs of individual children. Diagnostic teaching simply means that teachers employ observation, recording, and analysis of children's performance in day-to-day reading situations.

Diagnosis of Reading Readiness Skills Through Motor Learning

Reading readiness skills are a complex cluster of basic skills including (1) language development in which the child learns to transform his *experience* with his *environment* into language symbols through listening, oral language facility, and a meaningful vocabulary; (2) the skills relating to the mechanics of reading such as left-to-right orientation, auditory and visual discrimination, and recognition of letter names and sounds; and (3) the cognitive processes of comparing, classifying, ordering, interpreting, summarizing, and imagining.

Likewise, sensorimotor skills, meaning the functioning in both sensory and motor aspects of bodily activity, provide a foundation for these basic skills by sharpening the senses and developing motor skills involving spatial, form, and time concepts. The following list identifies some concepts developed through direct body movement inherent in motor learning. (The reader should notice that most of these items were discussed in Part II where they were concerned with improvement of learning ability through compensatory motor learning. They are repeated here for purposes of continuity and also because they have direct application for reading readiness.)

1. Body Awareness
2. Space and Direction
3. Balance
4. Basic Body Movements
5. Eye-Hand Coordination
6. Eye-Foot Coordination
7. Form Perception
8. Rhythm
9. Large Muscle Activity
10. Fine Muscle Activity

These skills are important to the establishment of a sound foundation for the beginning-to-read experiences of children. Not only can reading readiness experiences, structured for the development of these skills, be facilitated through motor learning situations, but diagnosis of progress in skill development can be obtained by teacher-child observation and a child's self-evaluation from the motor learning experiences. The following motor-learning situations are described to indicate a variety of motor learning experiences that may be used in the development and assessment of readiness skills.

Language Development

In the following motor learning experiences, concept formation is translated into meaningful vocabulary.

Concept: Vocabulary Meaning—Word Opposites
Activity: I'm Tall, I'm Small

Children stand facing each other a short distance apart. They walk around the activity area singing or saying the following verse:

> I'm tall, I'm very small,
> I'm small, I'm very tall,
> Sometimes I'm tall,
> Sometimes I'm small,
> Tell what I am now.

As the children walk around and sing "tall," "very tall," or "small," "very small," they stretch up or stoop down, depending on the words. At the end of the singing, they assume the position they were in at the time. If desired, a circle can be formed and one child stands in the center of the circle with eyes closed. The same procedure is followed, but at the end, the child in the center tries to guess the position of the others before opening his eyes.

This activity helps a child develop word meaning by acting out the words. Use of word opposites in this manner helps to dramatize the differences in the meaning of words. The words and actions can be changed to incorporate a large number of "opposites":

> My hands are near, my hands are far.
> Now they're far, now they're near,
> Sometimes they're near.
> Sometimes they're far.
> Tell what they are now.

Concept: Vocabulary Meaning—Action Words
Activity: What to Play

The teacher and children stand a few feet apart. The teacher acts as the leader and recites the following verse to the tune of "Mary Had a Little Lamb."

> (Name of child) tell us what to play,
> What to play, what to play,

(Name) tell us what to play,

Tell us what to play.

The teacher can then say "Let's play we're fish," or "Let's wash dishes," or any other thing that depicts action. The teacher performs the action and the children imitate.

This activity gives children an opportunity to act out meanings of words. It helps them to recognize that spoken words represent actions of people as well as things that can be touched.

Concept: Classification

Activity: Pet Store

One fairly large Pet Store is marked off at one end of the activity area and a Home at the other end. At the side is an area designated as a Cage. In the center of the playing area stands the Pet Store Owner. All of the players in the Pet Store are given a picture of one kind of pet (for example, fish, dog, cat, bird). These can be cut out of magazines or drawn by the teacher and children. There should be about two or three pictures of each kind of pet. The Pet Store Owner calls "Fish" (or any other pets in the game). The children who have the pictures of fish must try to run from the Pet Store to their new Home without being caught or tagged by the Owner. If they are caught, they must go to the Cage and wait for the next call. The game continues until all the Pets have tried to get to their new Home. Kinds of pets can be changed frequently.

By grouping themselves according to the animal pictures, children are able to practice classifying things that swim, things that fly, and so forth.

Auditory Discrimination

Concept: Auditory Discrimination—Beginning Sounds of Words

Activity: Man From Mars

One child is selected to be the Man from Mars and stands in the center of the activity area. The others stand behind a designated line at one end of the activity area. The game begins when the children call out, "Man from Mars, can we chase him through the stars?" The teacher answers, "Yes, if your name begins like duck" (or any other word). All the children whose names begin with the same beginning sound as *duck*, or whatever word is called, chase the Man from Mars until he is caught. The child who tags him becomes the new Man from Mars, and the game can continue.

For the children to run at the right time, they must listen carefully and match beginning sounds. If the teacher sees a child not running when he should, individual help can be given.

Concept: Auditory Discrimination—Auditory-Motor Association
Activity: I Say Stoop

The teacher stands facing the children a short distance away. The teacher says either "I say stoop" or "I say stand." The teacher carries out the action, but the children must carry out the command rather than the action. For example, if the teacher says, "I say stand" and stoops, a child, if he fails to follow the command rather than the action, could have a point scored against him if a score is kept. The position is reversed and a child is given a turn at being the leader.

Many opposite action or direction words could be used, such as in and out, stop and go, run and walk, up and down, forward and backward, and so on. This activity not only provides for alertness in auditory-motor association but also can give practice in recognition of word opposites.

Visual Discrimination

Concept: Visual Discrimination
Activity: Giant Step

The children stand at the back of a small area with a finish line a given distance away. The teacher uses pictures cut from magazines; if desired, these can be pasted on cards. The cards are of object pairs, similar and different. One pair of cards is held up. If the paired objects or symbols are the same, the children take a giant step forward. It should be observed to see the children's reaction if shown an unpaired set of cards. The winner is the one who gets to the finish line first.

Concept: Visual Discrimination
Activity: Match Cards

Each player in the group is given a different-colored card. Several players are given duplicate cards. There are two chairs placed in the center of the activity area. On a signal the players may walk, skip, etc. to musical accompaniment. When the music stops the teacher holds up a card. Those players whose cards match the teacher's card run to sit in the chairs. Anyone who gets a seat can be given a point. Play resumes and the cards should be exchanged frequently among the players.

DEVELOPING READING SKILLS THROUGH MOTOR LEARNING

For the most part, the development of successful reading ability is dependent upon the extent to which a child acquires various basic reading skills. There does not appear to be complete agreement among reading specialists on the terminology used to identify these basic reading skills. Neither do they agree entirely on how such skills should be classified. It has been my pleasure to collaborate on various projects with some of the most outstanding reading specialists in the United States. It is from these sources that I derive my descriptions of terminology and classifications. In this regard, it will be the intent of this section of the chapter to present motor learning situations that can be used effectively by teachers to develop skills in the areas of *sight vocabulary, word analysis,* and *comprehension.*

Sight Vocabulary

Sight vocabulary is concerned with being able to recognize a word on sight. Ordinarily, children may be expected to be able to identify a certain number of words on sight before they are introduced to the more complicated process of word analysis. However, there is a wide variation in recommendations of the number of sight words a child should acquire. This ranges from learning three or four words by sight to 100 or more words. Of course, this would be concerned with the age and ability level of each individual child.

The teacher should be aware that the learning of sight words involves *sounding;* thus, the importance of *saying* a word is emphasized. Some reading specialists go so far as to consider it as a *seeing, saying,* and *comprehending* process. The following motor learning experiences take these recommendations into account.

Concept: Sight Vocabulary
Activity: Find the Place

The teacher prepares a number of cards with a lettered word on each card. Let us say that on one of the cards is the word *chair.* The teacher holds up the card and calls out, "Chair!" The children run to a chair. If the children do not associate the object assistance can be given. The teacher might wish to give a clue such as "something to sit on." Many different kinds of words can be used.

Concept: Sight Vocabulary
Activity: Jump on the Word

The teacher takes a large piece of cloth such as an old bed sheet. Lines are drawn on the sheet to make six to nine sections. In each section a word is lettered. The children stand at the edge of the sheet. At the same time, the teacher calls out the word and a child tries to jump on it. For example, if the word is "tree," a picture of a tree is held up and the word is called out. As in the case of the previous activity, assistance can be given as needed. This activity also helps children associate picture clues with words.

Concept: Sight Vocabulary
Activity: Look for the Word

The same word cards for "Find the Place" can be used for this activity; however, a duplicate set is also needed. The teacher places the cards on the surface area with the children a short distance away. The teacher holds up a card and calls out the name of the word. The children run to the pile of cards to look for the word.

Concept: Sight Vocabulary
Activity: Word Carpet

The teacher prepares a list of words on a long piece of cardboard or portable chalkboard if one is available. Several individual pieces of cardboard with these words written on them are placed on the surface area to represent Word Carpets. The teacher gives a signal to "go" and the children skip around the surface area on the Word Carpets. When the teacher gives a signal to "stop," the teacher calls out the word and the children identify the word they are standing on or closest to from the list on the board.

Note: In the above activities the teacher should involve the children in saying the word and must decide in which way this will be most profitable. Teachers can derive words from children's stories and readers.

Word Analysis

The terms *word analysis, word recognition,* and *word attack* appear to be used interchangably to mean essentially the same thing when applied to the skills of reading. It should be understood that we cannot rely indefinitely upon sight vocabulary as a means of learning and remembering the literally thousands of words needed for reading. Therefore, efforts are made to begin rather early to develop skills that help the child learn vocabulary. Thus, it is the general function of word analysis skills to allow the child to progress faster in vocabulary development that would be the case if he had to learn each new word by sight.

Among other things, word analysis is concerned with such factors as letter recognition, auditory and visual discrimination, auditory-visual association, vowel letter patterns, syllabication, affixes, accent, and alphabetical order. Following are many suitable motor learning experiences that can be used to help in the development of word analysis skills.

Concept: Each sound has a definite form, and each form has a definite sound (auditory-visual perception)

Activity: Stop, Look, and Listen

Children stand a given distance away and facing the teacher. The teacher holds up a card with a letter of the alphabet. At the same time, the teacher calls out a word that *does* or *does not* begin with that sound. If the word does begin with the sound, the children run to where the teacher is standing. If the word does not begin with the sound, the children do not run. They try to see who can get there first.

Concept: Recognizing Letters of the Alphabet—Vowels

Activity: Magic Vowels

This activity is much like Word Carpet except that the "carpets" have vowels on them instead of words, and these are called Magic Vowels. At a signal to "go" the children skip around the Magic Vowels. At the signal to stop from the teacher the children try to name the vowel they are standing on. If able to do so they can be awarded a point with a certain number of points needed to complete the game. This activity can provide practice in the recognition of vowel letters.

Concept: Auditory Discrimination—Consonant Blends

Activity: Crows and Cranes

The playing area is divided by a center line. The players are divided into two teams. The players on one team are designated as Crows and take a position on one side of the playing area. The members of the other team are designated as Cranes and take a position on the other side of the playing area. The far baseline of each team is the safety zone. At the start the Crows and Cranes are about three feet apart. The teacher calls out "Cr-r-anes" or "Cr-rows." The initial consonant blend "Cr" is emphasized. If the teacher calls "Crows," they turn and run to their baseline to avoid being tagged. The Cranes attempt to tag their opponents before they cross their baseline. The Cranes score a point for each Crow tagged. They return to their places and the teacher proceeds to call one of the groups, and play continues in the same manner. The game can be extended to include other words beginning with consonant blends, for example, swans and swallows, storks and starlings, and squids and squabs.

Repetition of the consonant blends during the game helps children become aware of these sounds and to develop their auditory perception of the blends in the context of words. Discovering names of animals with other consonant blends can help children in their ability to hear consonant blends in the initial position of words.

Concept: Auditory Discrimination—Final Consonant Blends (*nk, ck, nd, st, nt, rst*)

Activity: Final Blend Change

The players form a single circle, with one player standing in the center of the circle. The players in the circle are designated as different final consonant blends. Each player may be given a card with his blend written on it to help him remember. The teacher then pronounces a word with one of the final position blends. All of the players with this blend must hold up their card and then run to exchange places. The player in the center tries to get one of the vacant places in the circle. The remaining player goes to the center. In this game, children must listen carefully to the word pronounced. By holding up their card, they are associating the visual with the auditory symbol for that sound.

Comprehension

As important as sight vocabulary and word analysis skills are in reading, the bottom line, so-to-speak, is comprehension. Without it, reading is reduced simply to the "calling of words." Many people have difficulty defining comprehension as it applies to reading. I like to think of it as the process of correctly associating meaning with word symbols, or simply extracting meaning from the written or printed page. Comprehension also involves evaluation of this meaning, sorting out the correct meaning, and organizing ideas as a selection is read. In addition, there should be retention of these ideas for possible use or reference in some future endeavor.

To accomplish comprehension as described here, it is important for children to develop certain comprehension skills. The following is a list of such *general* comprehension skills.

1. Getting Facts
2. Selecting Main Ideas
3. Organizing Main Ideas by Enumeration and Sequence
4. Following Directions
5. Gaining Independence in Word Mastery
6. Drawing Inferences
7. Building a Meaningful Vocabulary
8. Distinguishing Fact from Fantasy

The final section of the chapter, "Motor Learning Reading Content," will show how this list of comprehension skills can be used as an inventory for the teacher to evaluate how well a child is practicing and maintaining comprehension skills in listening and/or reading.

The following motor learning experiences are some representative ways in which one can assist children in developing comprehension. Some of the activities are concerned with general comprehension, while others are more specific in nature.

Concept: Vocabulary Meaning—On, Up, Down, Over, Under, Front, Back

Activity: Do What It Says

The teacher prepares word cards using the above words. The children respond to the sight of the word on the card and the calling of the word by the teacher. The teacher may say, "Go *under* the table," at the same time displaying the word card. The teacher can use the words in various ways depending upon the kind of objects and situations available in an inside or outside area where the activity takes place.

Concept: Following Directions

Activity: Simon Says

The teacher stands a given distance away, facing the children. To begin with, the teacher takes the part of Simon. Later these positions can be reversed so that the children get a turn at being Simon. Every time Simon says something, the children must do it. However, if a command is given without the prefix "Simon Says," the children must remain motionless. For example, when, "Simon says take two steps," the children must take two steps. But, if Simon says "Walk backward two steps," the children should not move. If desirable, some sort of scoring system can be devised to record the number of correct and incorrect responses.

This activity provides children the opportunity to follow oral directions in a highly motivating situation.

Concept: Following Directions
Activity: Do This, Do That

Cards with the words "Do This" and "Do That" are used in this activity. The teacher stands in front of the children a given distance away. The teacher holds up a card and makes a movement such as running in place or swinging the arms. The children follow the action of the teacher when the card says "Do This." When the teacher holds up the card sign that says "Do That," the children must not move although the teacher continues the action. Again, a point system can be devised if so desired, and the teacher and children can take turns at being the leader.

This activity can be used to help children to read carefully so as to follow directions. This game can be made more advanced later by having the teacher display written directions such as hop in place, jump once, run in place, etc.

Concept: Classification
Activity: Ducks Fly

The teacher stands in front of the children a given distance away. The teacher names different things that can fly such as ducks, birds, and airplanes. As the teacher calls out, "Ducks fly, Birds fly, Airplanes fly," he or she moves the arms as if flying. The children follow along as long as the teacher names something that can fly. If the teacher says "Elephants fly," and although the teacher continues to move the arms as in flying, the children must stop moving their own arms. If desired some sort of point system can be devised for scoring.

Children need to develop the skill of classifying things into groups having common characteristics. A child should be helped to notice that some animals actually can do several of the movements named as flying, walking, and/or swimming. This activity can be followed up by having the children collect pictures of animals and make a display of animals who walk, swim, etc.

MOTOR LEARNING READING CONTENT

The term *reading content* is easy to describe because it is simply concerned with the information that a given reading selection contains. Therefore, motor learning reading content provides for reading material that is oriented to motor learning situations. Stories of different length are prepared for various readability levels, and the content focuses upon any aspect of motor learning. Content can be concerned with such forms as active games, stunts, rhythmic activities, and creative experiences.

One of the early, and possibly the first, attempt to prepare motor learning reading content—at least as conceived here—is my own work, begun several years ago, and involving preparation of motor learning stories. These stories were used with several hundred children, and on the basis of the findings, the following generalizations were derived:

1. When a child is self-motivated and interested, he reads. In this case, the reading was done without the usual motivating devices such as picture clues and illustrations.
2. These motor learning stories were found to be extremely successful in stimulating interest in reading, and at the same time improving the child's ability to read.
3. Because the material for these motor learning stories was scientifically selected, prepared, and tested, it is unique in the field of children's independent reading material. The outcomes were most satisfactory in terms of children's interest in reading content of this nature as well as motivation to read.

From Listening to Reading

Before getting into the use of motor learning reading content, we need to take into account the important relationship between listening and reading. An important thing to remember is that the comprehension skills for listening are the same as the comprehension skills for reading (see previous list of comprehension skills). The essential difference in these two receptive phases of language is in the form of *input* that is used. That is, listening is dependent upon the *auditory* (hearing) sense, and reading is dependent upon the *visual* (seeing) sense. Since a main goal of reading is comprehension, it is important to recognize that as children listen to motor learning situations and react to them, they are developing essential skills for reading.

There seems to be solid evidence to support the idea that reading *to* children improves their vocabulary knowledge, reading comprehension, interest in reading, and the general quality of language development. I emphasize this at this point, because it will be seen later that reading to children is an important dimension in the use of motor learning reading content.

THE AMAV TECHNIQUE

The procedure for learning to read through the use of motor learning reading content is identified as the *AMAV Technique,* several examples of which will be presented later. The AMAV Technique involves a learning sequence of *auditory input* to *movement* to *auditory-visual input,* as depicted in the following diagram.

Auditory → *Movement* → *Auditory-Visual*

Essentially, this technique is a procedure for working through motor learning to develop comprehension first in listening and then in reading. The A → M aspect of AMAV is a directed listening-thinking activity. The child first receives the thoughts and feelings expressed in a motor learning story through the auditory sense by listening to the story being read. Following this, the child engages in the motor learning experiences that are inherent in the story, and thereby demonstrates understanding of and reaction to the story. By engaging in the motor learning experience, the development of comprehension becomes a part of the child's physical reality.

After the motor learning experience in the directed listening-thinking activity, the child moves to the final aspect of the AMAV Technique (A–V), a combination of auditory and visual experience by listening to the story read by the teacher and *reading along* with the teacher. In this manner, comprehension is brought to the reading experience.

Although the sequence of listening to reading is a natural one, bridging the gap to the point of handling the verbal symbols required in reading poses various problems for many children. One of the outstanding features of the AMAV Technique is that the motor learning experience helps to serve as a bridge between listening and reading by providing direct purposeful experience for the child through motor learning (movement) after listening to the story.

Following are several examples of stories that can be used in applying the AMAV Technique. Remember, first the story is read to the children and then with various degrees of guidance the children participate in the motor learning experience, and then the story is read by the children and teacher together.

THE FUNNY CLOWN

I am a funny clown.
I move like a funny clown.
I jump.
I skip.
I run.
I stop.
I have fun.

CIRCUS ELEPHANT

I saw the circus.
I saw many animals.
I saw an elephant.
He was big.
He had big legs.
He took big steps.
He had a trunk.
He swings his trunk.
I will walk like the elephant.

CURLY CAT TAKES A WALK

Curly Cat is asleep.
Curly opens his eyes.
Curly Cat takes a walk.
He walks with long steps.
He holds his head high.
He walks all around.
Try to walk like Curly Cat.
Put your hands on the floor.
Walk all around like Curly Cat.

GRIZZLY BEAR

I saw a grizzly bear.
Grizzly Bear was at the zoo.
He walked and walked.

He walked around his cage.
I can walk like Grizzly Bear.
I can put my hands on the floor.
I walk on my hands and feet.
I walk and walk.
I say, "Gr-Gr-Gr."

THE JUMPING RABBIT

I can jump like a rabbit.
I sit like a rabbit.
I hold my hands on the floor.
Now I jump.
My feet come up to my hands.
I hold my hands way out.
I put my hands on the floor.
I jump again.
I jump again and again.

THE SPIDER

Have you ever watched the way spiders walk?
They have long legs.
They put them way out.
Try to walk like a spider.
Put your hands on the floor.
Keep your arms straight.
Walk to the front.
Walk to one side.
Walk to the other side.
Walk to the back.
Walk all around like a spider.

THE LAME PUPPY

I saw a lame puppy.
The lame puppy walked.
He held up one leg.
He walked on three legs.
I walk like this puppy.
I hold up one leg.
I walk on one leg and two hands.
I walk around.

CASPER CAMEL

Casper Camel lives in the zoo.
He has a hump on his back.
Could you look like Casper Camel?
You will need a hump.
Try it this way.
Bend forward.
Put your hands behind your back.
Hold them together.
That will be a hump.
That will look like Casper Camel.
Could you move like Casper Camel.
Take a step.
Lift your head.
Take a step.
Lift your head.
Move like Casper Camel.

FALLING LEAVES

Leaves fall.
They fall from the trees.
They fall to the ground.
Fall like leaves.
Down, down, down.
Down to the ground.
Quiet leaves.
Rest like leaves.

THE GROWING FLOWERS

Flowers grow.
First they are seeds.
Be a seed.
Grow like a flower.
Grow and grow.
Keep growing.
Grow tall.
Now you are a flower.

ROCKING CHAIR (For two children)

There are many kinds of chairs.
One kind of chair is a rocking chair.
It rocks and rocks.
Two children can become a rocking chair.
They sit facing each other.
They sit on each other's feet.
They rock and rock.

SAMMY SQUIRREL (For several children)

One day Sammy Squirrel met some friends.
They wanted to run and play.
Sammy's friends went to one end of the field.
Sammy stayed in the center of the field.
He was *It.*
When Sammy said, "Change," his friends ran to the other end.
Sammy tried to tag them.
He tagged one.
Now he was Sammy's helper.
Sammy said "Change," again.
The squirrels ran back to the other end.
More squirrels were tagged.
They were Sammy's helpers.
Each time Sammy said, "Change," they ran to the other end.
They played until only one squirrel was left.
He was *It* for the next game.
Could you play this game with your friends?

Previously, I provided a list of general comprehension skills and indicated that I would show how this list could be used as an inventory to help the teacher determine how well the child is practicing and maintaining comprehension skills for listening and/or reading.

INVENTORY OF LISTENING AND/OR
READING COMPREHENSION SKILLS

Directions: Check YES or NO to indicate proficiency or lack of proficiency with which the child is using skills.

SKILLS

Yes	No		
____	____	1.	Getting Facts—Does the child understand what to do and how to do it?
____	____	2.	Selecting Main Ideas—Does the child use succinct instructions in preparing for and doing the motor learning activity?
____	____	3.	Organizing Main Ideas by Enumeration and Sequence—Does the child know the order in which the activity is performed?
____	____	4.	Following Directions—Does the child proceed with the activity according to the precise instructions in the story?
____	____	5.	Gaining Independence in Word Mastery—Does the child use word analysis to get a word without asking for help? (This applies only if the child has been introduced to word analysis skills.)
____	____	6.	Drawing Inferences—Does the child seem to draw reasonable conclusions as shown by the way he imitates the animal, person, or object in the story?
____	____	7.	Building a Meaningful Vocabulary—Does the child use any of the words in the story in his speaking vocabulary as he proceeds in the motor learning experience?
____	____	8.	Distinguishing Fact from Fantasy—Does the child indicate which stories are real and which are imaginary, particularly as far as some of the characters are concerned?

It should be recognized that different children will develop comprehension skills at different rates. Therefore, the teacher should be patient and provide cheerful teacher guidance as needed in assisting children in performing the motor learning experiences depicted in the stories.

It is entirely possible that some teachers will want to try to develop some of their own motor learning reading content, and I heartily recommend that they try their hand at it. Should this be the case, the following guidelines are submitted for consideration.

1. In general, the *new* word load should be kept relatively low.
2. When new words are used, there should be as much repetition of these words as possible and appropriate.
3. Sentence length and lack of complex sentences should be considered in keeping the level of difficulty of material within the ability levels of children.
4. Consideration must also be given to the reading values and literary

merits of a story. Using a character or characters in a story setting helps to develop interest.

5. The activity to be used in the story should *not* be readily identifiable. When children identify an activity early in the story, there can be resulting minimum attention on their part to get the necessary details to engage in the motor learning experience. Thus, in developing a motor learning story, it is important that the nature of the activity and procedures for it unfold gradually.

In closing this chapter, I want to emphasize that I have tried to show many possibilities available through which children can be helped with reading through the motor learning medium. It is hoped that these examples will inspire the reader to develop many additional experiences on his or her own.

Chapter 10

MATHEMATICS AND MOTOR LEARNING

O ver a long period of years there have been many periods of change
in mathematics in schools, and believe it or not, there was a time
when mathematics was not even considered a proper subject of study for
children. In the very early days of this country the ability to compute
was regarded as appropriate for a person doing menial work, but such
skill was not viewed as appropriate for the aristocracy. Accordingly, the
study of mathematics was not emphasized in the early schools of America,
not even the study of arithmetic.

Although over a period of many years changes in school mathematics
programs have been gradual, those changes since the mid-1950s have
been rather dramatic. These changes can be viewed as an acceleration of
the changes toward more mathematically meaningful instruction than
had taken place during the previous two decades, perhaps with a change
of focus. Several factors converged to help bring about the "revolution"
that occurred.

First of all, mathematics itself had changed, and attempts to unify
mathematical concepts led to new basic structures that had not yet been
reflected in mathematics instruction below the university level. Another
contributing factor was the accumulating information about how children learn, for it was becoming well established that children *could* learn
quite complex concepts, often at a younger age. Other factors often
cited include the concern that the mathematics curriculum was largely
the result of historical development rather than logical development, the
increasing need for an understanding of mathematics by people in
business and industry, and a belief on the part of many people that there
was an overemphasis on computational skills.

The elementary school mathematics programs that were developed
during the late 1950s and the 1960s focused heavily upon concepts and
principles and became immediately known as the *new math*. The content
of the programs for elementary school children contained more alge-
braic ideas and more geometry than had been included in previous

years. In addition, such things as relationships between operations were stressed.

When the *new math* was introduced into the American educational system it was probably one of the greatest upheavals in curriculum content and procedures up to that time. It also became the victim of much ridicule by educators and laymen alike. One night club entertainer was prompted to describe the purpose of the *new math* "to get the idea, *rather* than the right answer." One of my own mathematician friends, in comparing the *old math* and the *new math*, inferred that in the *old math* "they knew how to do it but didn't know what they were doing," whereas in the *new math*, "they know what they are doing but don't know how to do it."

In general, the *new math* was intended to do away with a process that had focused upon rote memory and meaningless computation. Further, it was expected that the new process would make it easier for students to develop mathematical understandings. The extent to which the *new math* achieved success was challenged by some laymen and by some educators as well. Obviously, most educational innovations have rightly been criticized when one gives consideration to the extremes that are possible in any educational process. Because of this, it now appears that attempts are being made to reach some sort of happy medium. While it is not likely that anyone wishes to revert entirely to the *old math*, at the same time, it would be desirable to avoid some of the extremes that have brought harsh criticisms of the *new math*.

It appears that present approaches to mathematics programs for children are such that they are being directed toward situations that are more suited to the everyday facts of life. It is my premise that the motor learning approach to learning about mathematics not only deals with the everyday facts of life, *but with life itself*—at least as far as the child is concerned.

MATHEMATICS READINESS

In the last chapter in the discussion of reading readiness it was indicated that it is a developmental stage at which certain factors have prepared the child for learning. Mathematics readiness can be viewed in this same general manner, since children should progress through certain developmental stages before they can be expected to be successful in the area of mathematics. For example, a child is probably not ready to take on the task of addition if he has to count objects to get a sum. Likewise, if he must add to find the product of two numbers, he is not yet ready for multiplication. Therefore, it seems that for the child to achieve mathematics readiness, time should be allowed for maturation of mental abilities and stimulation through experience. It might be said that *experience* is the key to the degree of mathematics readiness a child has attained upon entering school. In fact, research consistently shows that experience is a very important factor in readiness for learning in mathematics.

Because of experiences in mathematics—or lack thereof—children entering first grade vary a great deal in the amount of mathematical learnings they bring with them. It is becoming a common practice in many schools for teachers to try to determine how *ready* children are to deal with mathematics as they begin first grade. This gives the teacher an idea of the needs of the children and consequently serves as a basis for the teacher to group children with regard to instruction.

To give the reader some idea of how one might proceed, several *diagnostic* items in the area of mathematics are given here. (It should be clearly understood that these are not standard procedures, but merely representative examples of what teachers might do to help them determine how well acquainted the children are with some of the mathematical experiences that will be dealt with as they begin their formal education.)

Ordinarily, these items are administered orally with small groups of children. The teacher tries to observe certain behavior responses of children such as hesitation in answering, inattention, lack of ability in following directions, or anything that could be interpreted as immature thinking.

Generally speaking, teachers are concerned specifically with such features as counting, number symbols, number order, ordinal use of numbers, understanding of the simple fractions of ½, recognition of coins, and quantitative thinking.

The teacher might try to diagnose ability in *counting* by having children respond to such questions as the following: Can anyone count to find out how many boys there are in our class? Can anyone count to find out how many windows there are in our room? Can anyone tell us how many chairs we have? Can anyone tell how many pictures we have in our room? The teacher observes those children who volunteer and how correct their responses are. Different children are given an opportunity to answer the questions, and each time the responses are observed by the teacher.

In the *number symbols* area, a teacher might use a procedure like the following. Ten cards with each card having a number (1 to 10) are placed on the chalkboard tray. The teacher then asks questions such as: Who can find the card that tells us how many ears we have? What is the number? Who can find the card that tells us how many arms we have? What is the number? Which card tells us how many fingers we have on one hand? What is the number? Which card tells us how many doors there are in our room? What is the number?

In checking the children for their knowledge of *number order,* the same procedure is followed except that the card numbers are out of order. Such questions as the following may be asked: Can you help me put these cards in order? Another procedure used is to ask questions such as: What number comes right after 3? right after 6? right after 4? What is the number that comes right before 7? right before 10? right before 5? What is the number that comes between 1 and 3? between 6 and 8?

Ordinal numbers are used to show order or succession such as first, second, and so on. This can be diagnosed by placing number cards from 1 to 6 in order along the chalkboard tray. The teacher then may ask: Who can tell me the *first* card? the *fifth* card? the *third* card?

To help to determine how well the children understand the concept of one-half, the teacher can use six equal sized glasses. One glass can be full, one can be empty, and the rest of the glasses can be one-fourth full, one-third full, one-half full, and three-fourths full. Such questions as the following can be asked: Who can tell me which glass is full? Who can tell me which glass is empty? Who can tell me which glass is half full? Can you find a glass that is more than one-half full?

In diagnosing children's knowledge about *coins* the teacher will probably have about ten pennies, one nickel, and one dime. The teacher holds up each of the coins to see if the children can identify them. Such questions as the following can be asked: Does a penny buy less than a nickel? Does a dime buy more than a nickel? Which buys more, a penny or a dime? Would you give a nickel for four pennies? Would you give a dime for eight pennies?

Many of the motor learning experiences involving mathematics that are explained in the following sections of this chapter can be used to improve upon the child's mathematics readiness. Others are useful in helping a child with mathematics once he is in school.

MOTOR LEARNING EXPERIENCES INVOLVING NUMBERS

In using the term *number system,* I am referring to the base ten system of numeration (by tens, hundreds, thousands, and so on). Children first need to learn the meaning of 1, 2, 3, 4, 5, 6, 7, 8, and 9. Then they learn that there is a way of using these same numbers over and over again, with zero, to describe any number, regardless of how large it might be.

Catch a Bird Alive

This is a good idea for rote counting,* 1–10. The teacher and children stand on a starting line. They recite the following verse:

1, 2, 3, 4, 5,
I caught a bird alive;
6, 7, 8, 9, 10.
I let him go again.

The children and teacher count together, and as they count 1–5 they can take jumps forward. As they say the next phrase they pretend to catch a bird in their hands. They jump back to the original starting line as they count 6–10. As they say the last phrase they pretend to let the bird go.

In this activity a child gains skill in reciting the number names 1–10 in order, an essential skill in a child's early experiences with arithmetic.

Number Man

One player, the Number Man, faces the others, who are standing on a line at the end of a playing area. These players have counted off, starting with number 1, and each has a number. In the early stages of the activity it is a good idea to have the teacher play the part of the Number Man. The Number Man calls out "all numbers greater than ____." The players who have numbers greater than the one called must try to get to the other side of the playing area without being tagged by the Number Man. The Number Man may also call out "all numbers less than ____," "all even numbers," or "all odd numbers." Anyone who is tagged must help the Number Man tag the runners. Any child who runs out of turn is considered tagged.

In this activity children can gain skill with number sequence while

---

*Rote counting means counting from memory and rational counting means using reasoning when counting.

identifying numbers that are greater or less than a given number. When the players are lined up in sequence, it can be observed that the sets of odd numbers and even numbers involve every other whole number.

Call and Catch

The players stand in a circle, and each player is assigned a different number. The teacher throws a large rubber ball into the air and calls out a number by saying, "Just before four" or "Next after three." For example, if the teacher calls "Next after three," the player assigned the number four tries to catch the ball after it bounces.

In this activity a child can gain skill in using numbers in sequence. The teacher can help a child succeed in retrieving the ball by holding it momentarily after the number is called. As a child gains more mastery of the skill the ball can be tossed up at the same time the call is made.

Red Light

The teacher is *It* and stands a distance away from the children with his or her back to them. The teacher counts loudly, "10, 20, 30, 40, 50, 60, 70, 80, 90, 100, Red Light." The children advance toward the goal line as the teacher counts, but the children must stop when the teacher calls, "Red Light." As the teacher calls "Red Light" he or she turns, and if any children are moving they must return to the starting line. The object of the activity is to see which child reaches the goal line first.

This activity provides an opportunity for practice in counting by tens. Children have to anticipate the position of 100 in the sequence so as not to be caught off guard.

Come with Me

Players stand close together in a circle. One child is *It,* and he goes around the outside of the circle. *It* taps a player and says "Come with Me." That player follows *It. It* continues in the same manner, tapping players who then follow *It* as he goes around the outside of the circle. At any time *It* may call "Go Home." All the players following *It* run to find vacant places in the circle. The remaining player can be *It* when the activity continues. At the beginning the teacher has the children count how many there are. *It* can count the players as he taps them. All the players can also count as *It* taps the players. The number of players not tapped might also be counted.

The child, when *It,* is able to count varying-sized groups in this activity. By having the child who is *It* and the other players count as the players are tapped, he is helped to see the number names related to specific objects.

One, Two, Button My Shoe

The players stand toeing a line at one end of the activity area. One child is chosen as the leader and takes a position in front of the group. The group and the leader carry on the following dialogue:

Leader: One, two.
Group: Button my shoe.
Leader: Three, four.
Group: Close the door.
Leader: Five, six.
Group: Pick up sticks.
Leader: Seven, eight.
Group: Don't be late.

On the word *late* the players who were toeing the line run and try to reach another goal line a specified distance away, without being tagged by the leader. All players tagged become helpers for the next time, and the activity can continue until all are tagged. If desired the players can act out the dialogue as they say it.

This activity gives children practice in counting by ones and twos up to eight.

Airplane Zooming

The child jumps into the air and makes a one-quarter turn to his left. He does this three times until he has made a complete turn. The same procedure is repeated except that he turns to the right. A circle can be drawn on the surface area and divided into four parts. The child can stand in the center of the circle and jump from one quarter of the circle to the other. If desired, the teacher and child can call out together "one-quarter" and so on.

This is a good activity to help the child develop an understanding of the meaning of a whole number, one-half of a number, and one-fourth of a number.

MOTOR LEARNING EXPERIENCES
INVOLVING ARITHMETIC OPERATIONS

Certain motor learning experiences can provide the child with valuable experiences with the operations of arithmetic (addition, subtraction, multiplication, and division). The energetic involvement of children in the activities that follow brings an interest and enthusiasm to the learning of arithmetic operations that many children need very much.

Being a Number

This activity requires a minimum of six players. Players are given numbers of 1, 2, or 3 and dispersed around the playing area. They must remain in groups that do not add up to more than three. For example, three number 1s may be in a group, or a 1 and a 2, or a 3 alone. The players move around from one group to another and, at a given signal from the teacher, check to see that the groups add up to three. A number 1 can make a three by getting together with a 2. Three number 1s can get together to make three. At the signal, if a group totals more or less than three, a point can be scored against each person in the group, provided that it seems desirable to add more interest to the activity.

This activity gives an opportunity for addition of combinations 1 to 3. Also if a group has only two at the signal the teacher might ask, "How many more do you need to make three?" Or, if there are four in a group the question can be "How many less do you need to make three?" This brings in the idea of both addition and subtraction.

Fast Facts

The players are grouped according to a specific number to be thought of as a sum. As the activity begins, the players are lined up along a line on the activity area and clustered in their groups. Opposite each group on a parallel line is placed a marker or partition. The teacher calls out, "Four equals two plus two," and all the groups run to the other line. The players in a group arrange themselves so that two are on one side of the marker and two are on the other side. When all have agreed that the addition fact is correctly pictured, the teacher calls out, "Two plus two equals four," and all of the players run back to the starting line and form their groups again. The activity continues as the teacher calls out other addition facts for the same sum. If desired, a group can be given a point for being the first to picture the two addends.

A child can develop an understanding of the meaning of addition as he associates the partitioning of a set with various pairs of addends for a given sum. As a child interprets the orally given number sentences, he becomes more comfortable with the sum placed before the equal sign. The teacher should be alert to observe if a child is having difficulty including himself when counting the number of each part of the particular group of players.

Number Man (Variation)

Each player is assigned a number and stands behind a line at one end of the playing area. To start with, the teacher can be the Number Man. The Number Man calls out addition and subtraction problems such as "five plus six" and "twelve minus four." The players who have the number that is the answer (the missing sum or addend) for the problem must try to get past the Number Man to the line on the opposite side without being tagged. If tagged, the player must help the Number Man. As play continues, the children should be given the opportunity to be the Number Man.

In this activity reinforcement is provided for recalling missing addends and sums. This extra activity will help the child who may be having difficulty with this process.

Twice as Many

Players stand on a line near the end of the activity area. To begin with, the teacher can be the caller, who stands at the finish line 25 to 50 feet away. The caller gives directions such as "Take two hops. Now take twice as many. Take three small steps. Now take twice as many." Directions are varied in number and type of movement. Each direction is followed by "Now take twice as many." The first player to reach the finish line calls out, "Twice as many," and everyone runs back to the starting line. The caller tags all those he or she can before they reach the starting line. The caller tags all those he or she can before they reach the starting line. All those tagged help the caller for the next time.

The children are able to apply their knowledge of multiplication facts for the factor two in a highly motivation activity. The teacher may want to check each time a new direction is given to be sure children have multiplied by two accurately and have the correct answer.

Back to Back

Several partners stand back to back with arms interlocked at the elbows. The teacher points to each group and with the help of the players, counts by twos. If one player is left over, the number one is added and the total number of players is thereby determined. The teacher calls for any size group, and on a signal the players let go and regroup themselves in groups of the size called for. If the teacher calls for a group of two, the players must find a new partner. Each time the players are regrouped, they count by twos, threes, or whatever is appropriate, and add the number of players left over. (If the resulting number is not the total number of players, there has been an error, and groups should be counted again.) Whenever the number called for is larger than the group already formed, the teacher may choose to ask how many players are needed for each group to become the size group that has just been called for. Whatever the size group called for, the players must hook up back to back in groups of that number. A time limit may be set. The players who are left over may rejoin the group each time there is a call to regroup.

This activity not only provides experience with the multiples of a given factor but also informally prepares a child for uneven division. In fact, he may want to predict the number of players who will be left over before the signal to start regrouping is given. The teacher may choose to write number sentences to record each regrouping. For example, if there are nine players and groups of two have been called for, the record should show that four twos and one is nine or $(4 \times 2) + 1 = 9$.

Birds Fly South

Play begins with several players distributed randomly behind a starting line. The number of players is the dividend (or product). The teacher gives the signal to play by calling "Birds fly south in flocks of three" (or the largest divisor that will be used). The players run to another line that has been designated as "South." At this point the players should be grouped in threes. After observing the number of flocks (the quotient), the players who remain (that is, those who were not able to be included in one of the flocks) become hawks, who take their places between the two lines. Then with the call "Scatter! the hawks are coming!" the players run back to the other line, with the hawks attempting to tag them. Note is taken of who is tagged. Play continues, with the players taking their place behind the starting line. The teacher then uses the next lower number for the call. If three was used first, two would be called next. "Birds fly south in flocks of two." This continues until groups of two have been formed and they return to the starting line. Each time the number of flocks that are formed should be observed.

This activity is concerned with the meaning of division and the effect of increasing or decreasing the divisor. At the end of the activity the teacher should consider the arithmetic that has been applied. If possible, the teacher can record division number sentences showing the number of flocks formed when different divisors were used for the same dividend. A child should be helped to form the generalization that, for a given dividend (product), when the divisor (known factor) decreases, the quotient (unknown factor) increases in value. After this pattern is established, the number called can be reversed, beginning with the smallest divisor and working up to the highest divisor to be used. Here, the opposite of the previous statement can be developed.

Take Away, Take Away

This rhythmic activity requires a minimum of five players who stand in a circle. One child is *It.* He walks around the inside of the circle. As the players sing the following song, to the tune of "Twinkle Twinkle Little Star," they act out the words of the song.

> Take away, take away, take away one.
> Come with me and have some fun.
> Take away, take away, take away two.
> Come with me, oh yes please do.
> Take away, take away, take away three.
> All please come and skip with me.

It taps one player. This player follows behind *It. It* then taps a second and third player. At the end of the song all three players try to get back to their places in the circle. *It* also tries to get into one of the vacant places. The remaining player can be *It* for next time.

This activity enables a child to see demonstrated the concept of subtraction. The teacher may have a child identify how many players are left each time *It* takes away one player.

Dance Around the Ring

This rhythmic activity requires nine players. Three of the players stand together. Then three more players stand together. Finally, the last three players stand together so that groups of three can be distinguished. The nine players all join hands and make a ring (circle). They sing this song to the tune of "Rock-A-Bye-Baby."

> If you take three and add on three more.
> You will have six you know I am sure.
> Again you add three and now you will find
> That with these three threes you now have nine.

The song is sung through three times. When it is sung the first time the players walk around the ring. When it is sung the second time they walk into the center of the ring and back. The third time the song is sung they skip around the ring. The players are asked to think about the numbers as they do the activity.

This activity involves the idea that multiplication is a short way to add. It also provides an understanding that there can be *sets* of something, in this case sets of three people. The multiplication concept can be developed with the children as three groups of three are seen; that is, three threes make nine. As the players get together it can be pointed out that they make a group of three.

MOTOR LEARNING EXPERIENCES INVOLVING OTHER AREAS OF MATHEMATICS

Thus far, number, numeration, and the operations of arithmetic have been the mathematical concepts and skills that have been related to motor learning experiences. We now turn our attention to various other areas of mathematical learnings that children can come to understand through this medium. These involve geometric figures, linear and liquid measurements, telling time, and recognition of coins and their values.

It is interesting to note that one of these areas—that which is concerned with learning about basic geometric patterns—can be beneficial to the child in other educational pursuits as well as mathematics. This is concerned with the child's beginning efforts to learn to write. Beginning writing experiences involve circles, parts of circles, and straight lines, which of course, are geometric figures.

Show a Shape

The children stand a short distance away from the teacher, who calls, "Take two turns and show a ___," specifying the two-dimensional geometric figure the children are to form with arms or body. The children turn around twice, then form the figure named. For example, a circle can be suggested easily with both arms overhead as hands touch. By bending elbows but keeping hands and forearms rigid, different quadrilaterals can be formed. A child who touches his toes while keeping his legs straight makes a triangle. At times the teacher and children can work together to form other figures.

Lines, line segments, rays, and angles can also be shown. A child can let his extended arms represent a part of a line, with a fist used to suggest the end point. An infinite extension can be suggested by pointing the finger. For angles, the torso can become the vertex as the arms are swung to different positions. Acute, right, and obtuse angles can all be pictured in this way. Of course, a child without previous experience will need to be given instructions in the movement before the activity is performed.

This activity can help a child learn that geometric figures are not just marks on paper, that they consist of a set of locations in space. The activity can be used to introduce selected definitions, for example, an obtuse angle. However, because many of the figures formed will be suggestive rather than precise, the activity will usually be used for reinforcement.

Jump the Shot

This activity has been described elsewhere in the book (see p. 96).

This activity can be used to help the child visualize not only the circle itself but the radius of a circle as well. The child should be helped to understand that the rope, which represents the radius, is the same length from the center to any point along the circle.

Run Circle Run

Several players form a circle by holding hands and facing inward. Depending on the size of the group, players count off by twos or threes (for small groups) or fours, fives, or sixes (for large groups). The teacher calls one of the assigned numbers. All of the players with that number start running around the circle in a specified direction; each runner tries to tag one or more players running in front of him. As a successful runner reaches his starting point without being tagged, he stops. Runners who are tagged go to the interior of the circle. Another number is called and the same procedure is followed. This continues until all have been called. The circle is reformed, new numbers are assigned to the players, and the activity is repeated. As the number of players decreases, a smaller circle can be drawn on the surface inside the larger circle; the players must stay out of the smaller circle when running around to their places.

This activity deals with the concept that a circle is a simple, closed curve, and also the interior of the circle. The teacher should help a child to see that when the players form a circle by holding hands, they make a continuous, simple, closed shape. As they engage in the activity it can be observed what happens to the size of the circle as parts of it break off. It can also be learned that the space within the circle is called the interior of the circle.

Inside Out

The players divide into groups of four or more. Players on each group join hands to form a circle in which each player faces toward the inside. When the teacher calls "inside out," each group tries to turn its circle inside out; that is, while *continuing* to hold hands, the players move so as to face out instead of in. To do this, a player will have to lead his group under the joined hands of two group members. The first group to complete a circle with players facing toward the outside of the circle can be declared the winner.

This activity is designed as a kind of puzzle or problem-solving activity, for the goal is presented to the players and they are not told how it is possible to turn the circle inside out. It is designed to be the initial encounter with the process involved.

Add-a-Jump

The children serve as their own scorekeepers. They stand on a starting line. A child steps on the starting line and jumps as far as he can. Other children do likewise. The children mark where they landed. Each then measures the distance he or she jumped. If desired, several jumps can be taken by each, and the distance of all jumps can be added.

This activity can use linear measurement, figuring an average or mean, and addition, including decimals. In addition to developing measuring skills, this activity provides practice and experience in comparing distances. Either English or metric units can be used for measuring. An average or mean can be determined by adding the distance of all jumps and dividing by the number of jumps.

Milkman Tag

Two groups of three milkmen are selected and given milk truck bases. One group might be called Chocolate, the other White. The remaining players are called Pints. On a given signal, one milkman from each group tries to tag any of the Pints. When he tags one they both go to the milk truck, and another milkman goes after a Pint. The players must figure out how many Pints will be needed to make the necessary number of quarts.

A child is provided with a highly motivating activity for applying the idea of liquid measurement that two pints are equivalent to one quart. Players may want to group Pints in twos to determine how many quarts each group has.

Tick Tock

Players form a circle that represents a clock. Two players are runners, and they are called Hour and Minute. The players chant, "What time is it?" Minute then chooses the hour and calls it out (six o'clock). Hour and Minute must stand still while the players in the circle call "One o'clock, two o'clock, three o'clock, four o'clock, five o'clock, six o'clock" (or whatever time is chosen). When the players get to the chosen hour, the chase begins. Hour chases Minute clockwise around the outside of the circle. If Hour can catch Minute before the players in the circle once again call out "One o'clock, two o'clock, etc." (the same hour is counted the first time), he chooses another player to become Hour. The activity can also be played by counting half hours.

A child not only gets practice in calling the hours in order, but he also gains experience with the concept of the term *clockwise*.

Double Circle

Players are arranged in a double circle. The outside circle has one more player than the inside circle. The players in both circles skip around to their right (each circle goes in the opposite direction) until a signal is given to stop. Each player then tries to find a partner from the other circle. The player left without a partner is said to be "in the doghouse." Play can continue as long as desired.

This activity is good to develop the idea of time-telling terminology—
clockwise and counter clockwise.

Cobbler, Cobbler

Players form a circle, with one player in the center. The player in
the center holds an object that is supposed to represent a shoe. As the
following verse is recited, the player in the center passes the "shoe" to
another in the circle.

> Cobbler, cobbler
> Mend my shoe.
> Have it done by
> Half-past two.

The shoe is then passed behind the backs of the players during the
reciting of the next verse, which is as follows:

> Sew it up or
> Sew it down.
> Now see with whom
> The shoe is found.

On the word "found" the player who has the shoe becomes *It* and goes to
the center of the circle.

This activity can develop an understanding of telling time by the
half-hour. The players may make up other verses, using other half-hour
intervals, such as half-past three, half-past four, and so on.

Bank

This activity can be conducted with a small number of players, and
even two players could do the activity if desired. A child is selected to be
the Bank. The rest of the players stand at a starting line about 20 feet
away from the Bank. The Bank calls out a number of pennies, nickels, or
dimes a player may take. (A penny is one small step, a nickel equals five
penny steps, and a dime equals ten penny steps: hopping and jumping
can also be used instead of steps.) The Bank calls a player's name and
says, "George, take three pennies." George must answer "May I?" The
Bank then says "Yes, you may" or "No, you may not." If George forgets to
say "May I?" he must return to the starting line. The first player to reach
the Bank becomes the Bank for the next time. All players should have a
chance to be the Bank.

By taking the steps forward toward the Bank, a child can gain an understanding that a nickel has the same value as five pennies and a dime has the same value as ten pennies.

Banker and the Coins

Each player is given a sign to wear, which denotes one of the following: five cents, ten cents, twenty-five cents, fifty cents, nickel, dime, quarter, or half-dollar. To start the activity, a child can be the Banker. He calls out different amounts of money up to one dollar. The players run and group themselves with the other players until their group totals the amount of money called by the Banker. All players should have a chance to be the Banker.

A child can gain practice in combining different amounts of money to arrive at a specific amount. He can learn that there are usually several different ways one can combine coins to produce a specified amount of money. The teacher checks that a group is correct, and the whole group can count it out. In this way, a child will be more likely to learn about values of coins if he is unsure.

THE MATHEMATICS MOTOR LEARNING STORY

The widespread success resulting from the use of motor learning reading content reported in the previous chapter inspired the development of the same general type of reading content that would also include mathematics experiences. This kind of reading content was arbitrarily called the *mathematics motor learning story.*

Early attempts to develop mathematics motor learning stories were patterned after the original procedure used in providing for motor learning reading content; that is, several stories were written around motor learning experiences, the only difference being that the content also involved reference to mathematics experiences. These stories were tried out in a number of situations. It soon became apparent that with some children the understanding of the mathematics concepts in the story was too difficult. The reason for this appeared to be that certain children could not handle the task of reading while at the same time developing an understanding of the mathematics aspect of the story. It was then decided that since *listening* is a first step in learning to read, auditory input should be used. This procedure involved having a child or children listen to a story, perform the activity, and simultaneously try to develop the mathematics concept. When it appeared desirable, this process was extended by having children try to read the story after having engaged in the activity. Thus, the first recommendation would be to have the teacher simply read the story to the child or children. If it seemed practical under the particular circumstances then the AMAV technique referred to in the previous chapter could be used.

Several experiments with the mathematics motor learning story have shown somewhat conclusively that children can benefit from this listening experience and develop the mathematics concept in the story as well. The following discussion is an example of an experiment of this approach with a group of 30 children. The name of the story is "Find a Friend," and it is an adaptation of the activity "Busy Bee." The mathematics concepts in this story are *groups or sets of two; counting by twos; beginning concepts of multiplication.*

FIND A FRIEND

In this game each child finds a friend.
Stand beside your friend.
You and your friend make a group of two.
One child is *It.*
He does not stand beside a friend.
He calls, "Move!"
All friends find a new friend.

It tries to find a friend.
The child who does not find a friend is *It.*
Play the game.
Count the number of friends standing together.
Count by two.
Say, "Two, four, six."
Count all the groups this way.

The group of first grade children with which this experiment was conducted bordered on the remedial level (slow learners) and had no previous experience in counting by twos. Before the activity, each child was checked for this ability. Also, the children had no previous classroom experience with beginning concepts of multiplication.

The story was read to the children and the directions were discussed. The game was demonstrated by the experimenter and several children. Five pairs of children were used at one time. As the game was being played, the activity was stopped momentarily, and the child who was *It* at the moment was asked to count the groups by twos. The participants were then changed, the number participating changed, and the activity was repeated.

In evaluating the experiment it was found that this was a very successful experience from a learning standpoint. Before the activity, none of the children were able to count by twos. A check following the activity showed that 18 of the 30 children who participated were able to count rationally to 10 by twos. Seven of the children were able to count rationally to six, and two were able to count to four. Three children showed no understanding of the concept. No attempt was made to check beyond ten because in playing the game the players were limited to numbers under ten.

There appeared to be a significant number of children who had profited from this experience in a very short period of time. The teacher of the group maintained that in a more conventional teaching situation, the introduction and development of this concept with children at this low level of ability would have taken a great deal more teaching time, and the results would have been attained at a much slower rate.

Following are several mathematics motor learning stories that have been used with success. The story should be read to the child or group as the case may be, and then the directions of the story are discussed. This is followed by participation in the activity with an attempt being made to develop an understanding of the mathematics concept(s) in the story. Each story is accompanied with an identification of the concepts along with suggestions as to how the concepts might be developed.

JUMP AWAY

In this game children jump.
Six players stand in a line.
One player jumps away.
Now there are five players.
Another jumps away.
Now there are four.
Another jumps away.
Now there are three.
Another jumps away.
Now there are two.
Another jumps away.

Now there is one.
That player jumps away.
Now all have jumped away.

Mathematics Skills and Concepts: subtraction through six; taking away one; geometric figure (line)
Suggestions:

1. The teacher can call attention that the players are standing in a line. A line could be drawn to help in the understanding of this geometric figure.
2. The teacher can ask the players who jump away to call out how many there are left as he jumps, or after he jumps. If he does not know he can turn around and count the number.
3. The teacher may wish to put the subtraction facts through six on flash cards and use them in connection with the activity. This might be an evaluative technique for a child after participation in the activity.

JUMP AND TURN

Stand straight.
Put your feet together.
Jump up.
Turn as you jump.
Now you are looking the other way.
You are halfway around.
Jump again.
Now you are back again.
You are all the way around.
You jumped around.
You took two jumps.

Mathematics Skills and Concepts: vocabulary (half and whole); addition of fractions (two halves make a whole).
Suggestions:

1. The teacher can show the child that he made two jumps to get the "whole" way around.
2. Two half circles can be drawn on the surface area or made out of cardboard as an example of two halves. When the child takes the first jump he has made the first half circle and with the second jump the second half, making the whole circle.

HOP AND JUMP

Stand straight.
Now stand on one foot.
Hop on this foot.
Hop again.
Now stand on both feet.
Jump on both feet.
Jump four times.
Tell how many times you hopped.
Tell how many times you jumped.
Tell how many more times you jumped.
Tell how many fewer times you hopped.

Mathematical Skills and Concepts: addition; subtraction; rational counting; inequality of numbers (more than, less than)
Suggestions:

1. Have the child count as he hops and jumps.
2. The activity can be repeated a number of times using different combinations.
3. For a child who may have difficulty remembering how many more or how many fewer, one footprint can be drawn on a piece of cardboard to represent a hop and two footprints can be drawn on a piece of card to represent a jump. The child can be given the cardboard and he can trace his own feet.

MRS. BROWN'S MOUSE TRAP

(Gender can be changed as necessary—Mr. or Mrs.)
Some of the players stand in a circle.
They hold hands.
They hold them high.
This will be a mouse trap.
The other players are mice.
They go in and out of the circle.
One player will be Mrs. Brown.
She will say, Snap!"
Players drop hands.
The mouse trap closes.
Some mice will be caught.
Count them.

Tell how many.

Tell how many were not caught.

Mathematics Skills and Concepts: rational counting; addition; subtraction
Suggestions:

1. All of the players can count together the number caught.
2. All of the players can count together the number not caught.
3. If the teacher wishes, the players who are caught can stand in a line facing those not caught. This way the difference can easily be seen.

HOP ALONG

Hop on one foot.

Now hop on the other foot.

Hop two times on your left foot.

Hop six times on your right foot.

You hopped more times on your right foot.

Tell how many more.

Mathematics Skills and Concepts: addition; subtraction; rational counting; vocabulary (left and right); inequality of numbers (more than)
Suggestions:

1. Have a child count as he hops.
2. The teacher can put the number of hops on flash card to show the difference.
3. Left and right footprints can be drawn on the surface area or cardboard, and if the child has difficulty with right and left he can hop on one of these.

RUN ACROSS

The players stand in a line.

They stand beside each other.

One player is *It.*

The player who is *It* goes in front of the line.

He calls, "Run!"

The players run to the other end.

It tags as many as he can.

Tell how many were tagged.

Tell how many were left.

The players who were tagged help *It.*

Again *It* calls, "Run!"

More are tagged by *It* and his helpers.
Tell how many were tagged.
Tell how many were left.
Play until all but one is tagged.
He can be *It* for next time.

Mathematics Skills and Concepts: addition; subtraction; rational counting; geometric figure (line)
Suggestions:

1. All the players can count together the number tagged.
2. All the players can count together the number left.
3. The players tagged can stand in a line facing those who were left. This way the difference can easily be seen.
4. The teacher can call attention that they are standing on a line. A line could be drawn to help them understand the geometric figure.

SING AND TAP

It takes seven players to do this song and dance.
Six of the players hold hands to make a circle.
One player stands in the circle.
Now everyone sings this song.
Sing it to the tune of "London Bridge is Falling Down."

One plus two plus three make six.
All make six, all make six.
Three plus two plus one make six.
Make six also.

The six players walk around the circle as they sing.
The other player walks around in the circle.
The players stoop down when the song ends.
The player in the circle tries to tag someone.
He tries to tag a player before he gets down.
Think of the numbers as you sing.
$1 + 2 + 3 = 6, 3 + 2 + 1 = 6.$
Think of how they are changed but still make six.

Mathematics Skills and Concepts: commutative law (the sum is the same regardless of the order); addition
Suggestions:

1. To reinforce the understanding of commutative law the teacher can

put 1 + 2 + 3 = 6 and 3 + 2 + 1 = 6 on flash cards before and/or after the activity.

2. The above procedure can also be used for the addition combinations.

GO UP AND DOWN

Let's stand facing each other.
Now let's hold hands.
Now you stoop down.
Now you stand and I'll stoop down.
Let's count as we go up and down.
You say, "One."
I'll say, "Two."
Let's go up and down 10 times.
You will say, "1, 3, 5, 7, 9."
You will be counting by odd numbers.
I will say, "2, 4, 6, 8, 10."
I will be counting by even numbers.
Maybe we will be able to do it more times counting the same way.

Mathematics Skills and Concepts: odd and even numbers' counting by twos.

Suggestions:

1. After children go up and down together, one child can do it alone counting by twos as he does it.
2. The starting position can be changed so that the children have both odd and even numbers.

A STUNT WITH FOUR PARTS

Here is a stunt with four parts.
First you stand straight with feet together.
Hands are at your side.
Next you stoop down to a squat position.
Your hands are in front on the ground.
Now you have done the first part of the stunt.
You have done 1/4 of the stunt.
Next you kick your legs way back.
Now you have done 1/2 of the stunt.
Next you bring your legs back to the squat position.
Now you have done 3/4 of the stunt.
Now you stand up straight again.

Now you have done the whole stunt.

You can do it as many times as you like.

Mathematics Skills and Concepts: fractional parts of a whole ($1/4$, $1/2$, $3/4$); addition of fractions

Suggestions:

1. The teacher can make a circle out of cardboard and cut it into fourths. As the child does each part of the stunt the fourths can be put together.
2. Another variation would be to draw a circle on the surface area. The child makes his jumps in the circle, calling out the fractional part as he jumps.

As suggested in the previous chapter, teachers may want to try to develop their own original stories. The reader is referred back to the guidelines given in Chapter 9 for assistance in this endeavor.

Chapter 11

SCIENCE AND MOTOR LEARNING

The opportunities for science experiences through motor learning are so numerous that it is difficult to visualize a motor-oriented experience that is not related to science in some way. Indeed, the possibilities of a better understanding of science and the application of science principles in motor learning activities are almost unlimited.

Although the main purpose of this chapter is to deal with *specific* ways to learn about science through motor learning activities, some mention should be made about how this can occur *generally*.

GENERAL WAYS OF USING
MOTOR LEARNING ACTIVITIES IN SCIENCE

The following generalized list is submitted to give the reader an idea of some of the possible ways in which opportunities for science experiences might be utilized through various kinds of motor learning activities.

1. The physical principle of *equilibrium* or state of balance is one that is involved in many motor learning activities. This is particularly true of *stunt* activities in which balance is so important to proficient performance.
2. *Motion* is obviously the basis for all motor learning activities. Consequently, there is opportunity to relate laws of motion, at least in an elementary way, to movement experiences of children.
3. Children may perhaps understand better the application of *force* when it is thought of in terms of hitting a ball with a bat or in tussling with an opponent in a combative stunt.
4. *Friction* may be better understood by the use of a rubber-soled gym shoe on a hard-surfaced playing area.
5. Throwing or batting a ball against the wind can show how *air friction* reduces the speed of flying objects.
6. Accompaniment for rhythmic activities such as the drum, piano,

and recordings help children to learn that *sounds* differ from one another in pitch, volume, and quality.

7. The fact that *force of gravitation* tends to pull heavier-than-air objects earthward may be better understood when the child finds that he must aim above a target at certain distances.

8. Ball-bouncing presents a desirable opportunity for a better understanding of *air pressure*.

9. Weather might be better understood on those days when it is too inclement to go outside to the activity area. In this same connection, weather and climate can be considered with regard to the various sport seasons—that is baseball in spring and summer, and games that are suited to winter play and cold climates.

It should be understood that the above represents just a partial list of such possibilities, and a person with just a little ingenuity could expand it to a much greater length.

MOTOR LEARNING ACTIVITIES IN WHICH SCIENCE CONCEPTS ARE INHERENT

Several areas in the study of childhood science are included here. These are (1) the earth and universe, (2) conditions of life, and (3) physical and chemical changes. In each area a number of science concepts are presented with motor learning experiences in which these concepts are inherent. Descriptions of the activities along with suggestions for use are included.

The Earth and Universe

Concept: Planets' orbit around the sun.
Activity: Planet Ball

The children form a single circle and count off by twos. The number ones step forward, turn and face the number twos. The larger circle should be about four feet outside the inner circle. Two children, designated as team captains, stand opposite each other in the circle. The teacher stands in the center of the circle and represents the sun. Each captain has a ball that his team identifies as a planet. On a signal from the teacher, each ball is passed counterclockwise to each team member until it travels all the way around the circle and back to the captain. Any child who is responsible for the ball striking the floor, either through a poor throw or failure to catch the ball, has to recover the ball. As both circles pass the balls simultaneously, the time is kept and recorded. The group that passes the ball around its circle first wins or scores a point. Groups should exchange positions every several rounds.

Suggested Use: Prior to playing the game, the children should notice that the balls being passed around are the planets and that they are revolving around the sun represented by the teacher. They should be helped to identify the balls that are being passed counterclockwise because that is the direction the planets orbit the sun. In using this activity to illustrate the orbits of planets, it should be stressed that the path or orbit of the ball should be unbroken or uninterrupted. It should also be noticed that each completed orbit was done with different amounts of time for each circle, and that the inner circle tended to take less time to pass the ball around. Children can be encouraged to find out the differences in the orbits of the planets as well as the varying lengths of times of these orbits.

Concept: Earth's orbit around the sun
Activity: Earth's Orbit Relay

The children are arranged in two circles, each circle facing in. A captain is selected for each team, and they stand ready with balls in their hands. On a signal, each captain starts his team's ball around by passing to the child on his right. Upon receiving the ball each child spins around and passes the ball on to the next child on the right. As the ball makes a complete circuit back to the captain, he calls, "One!" The second time around he calls "Two!" This procedure is repeated until the first team to pass the ball around the circle five times wins.

Suggested Use: In this activity the children need to be helped to see they are dramatizing the way the earth revolves around the sun. The entire circle becomes the complete orbit of the earth. The ball represents the earth, and as it is passed from one child to another, they can see how the earth revolves around the sun. Also, since each child must spin around with the ball before passing it on, the concept of earth's rotation on its axis may be shown. The children must always run and pass counterclockwise since that is the direction of the earth's orbit.

Concept: The turning of the earth on its axis causes day and night.
Activity: Night and Day

The children stand in a circle holding hands. One child in the center of the circle represents the earth. As the children hold hands, they chant,

Illery, dillery, daxis,
The earth turns on its axis.
Isham, bisham bay,
It turns from night to day.

While the children are chanting, earth closes his eyes and turns slowly with one hand pointing toward the circle of children. As he rotates slowly with eyes closed (night), he continues to point with his hand. At the word *day* he stops and opens his eyes (day). Earth then runs after the child to whom he is pointing at the word *day;* they run around the outside of the circle until he catches him. When the child is caught, he becomes the new earth. The original earth joins the circle and the game continues. It might be advisable to use a blindfold that the child can slip off at the end of the verse.

Suggested Use: The child in the center becomes the rotating earth. When his eyes are closed it becomes night, and when his eyes are open it becomes day. The children might be encouraged to think of the child being pointed to as the sun since it is day when the eyes are opened, and the sun causes day.

Concept: Eclipse of the moon.
Activity: Eclipse Tag

The children are grouped by couples facing each other. The couples are scattered in any way about the activity area. One child is chosen for the runner and is called the earth. Another child is the chaser. On a signal, the chaser tries to tag earth. Earth is safe from being tagged when he runs and steps between two children who make up a couple. When earth steps between the two children he calls out, "Eclipse!" The chaser must then chase the child in the couple toward whom earth turns his back. If the chaser is able to tag earth, they exchange places.

Suggested Use: This activity enables children to dramatize the concept of an eclipse of the moon so that they can see what occurs. The children should be helped to identify that when earth steps between two children, the one he faces is the moon and his back is turned to the sun, and that the earth's shadow covers the moon.

Concept: Force of gravity
Activity: Catch the Cane

The children are arranged in a circle, facing in. Each child is given a number. One child becomes *It* and stands in the center of the circle. He holds a stick or bat upright and balances it by putting his finger on the top of it. *It* calls one of the numbers assigned to the children in the circle. At the same time, he lets go of the stick. The child whose number is called dashes to get the stick before it falls to the ground. *It* dashes to the place occupied by the child whose number was called. If the child gets the stick in time then he returns to his place in the circle, and *It* holds the stick again. After the children have learned the game, several circles can be formed to provide active participation for more children. The teacher can provide for individual differences of poor performers by making the circle smaller.

Suggested Use: The stick in this game represents the object which is being acted upon by the force of gravity. Every time *It* lets go of the stick, the stick begins to fall to the ground. This demonstrates the concept of the force of gravity to children. They may be helped to notice that they must move faster than the force of gravity in order to catch the stick before it falls to the ground.

Concept: Force of gravity.
Activity: Jump the Shot
   This activity has been described elsewhere in the book (see p. 155).
   Suggested Use: The game is played in small groups, and each child should have a turn to be in the center and swing the rope. The teacher might ask the children what they felt on the other end of the rope as they swung it around—that is if they felt a pull. The teacher can ask what would happen if the rope broke or if they let go of their end. This can be demonstrated. Further questions can lead to what kept the rope and beanbag from flying off during the game, what the inward pull was on the rope that kept the beanbag moving in a circular pattern. The teacher might also relate this to the manner planets travel in a circular orbit around the sun and the moon circles the earth because of gravitational force.

Concept: Gravitational pull—of tides, planets.
Activity: Planet Pull (Tide Pull)
   The children are divided into two teams. One can be named earth and the other, moon. The first child on each team kneels down on all fours, facing a member of the other team. There is a line drawn on the floor between them. Each child has a collar made from a towel or piece of strong cloth placed around his neck. Each child grabs both ends of the other person's towel. The object is for each one to try to pull the other one across the line. The child who succeeds scores a point for his team.

Each child on the team does the same. The team with the most points wins.

Suggested Use: This activity can be used to demonstrate the gravitational pull of earth and the moon, or the planets and the sun. It might be pointed out that a larger child was often stronger and was usually able to pull a smaller child across the line just as members of the solar system are pulled to the largest member, the sun.

Concept: Earth's atmosphere—air has pressure and pushes against things.
Activity: Balloon Throw

Children take turns throwing an inflated toy balloon. A line is marked on the floor, and the thrower may use any method of throwing as long as he does not step on or over this line. His Throw is measured from the line to the spot his balloon first touches the floor. The child with the longest throw wins.

Suggested Use: The children can experience the feeling of throwing an object so light in relation to size that the resistance of air prevents the object from traveling in an arc as expected. In substituting a playground ball, the children can notice the difference in the distance it travels in the same type of throw. A tennis ball can also be used for comparison of distance traveled and action of throwing.

Concept: Earth's atmosphere—force of lift of air.
Activity: Air Lift

The children are divided into teams of four to six members each. One team stands on one side of a net stretched across the center of the court. The size of the court may vary. The game is started by one child throwing a rubber ring over the net. Any opposing team member may catch the ring and throw it back. The ring may not be relayed to another child on the same team. Play continues until a point is scored. A point is made each time the ring hits the ground in the opponents' court or when any of the following fouls are committed:

1. Hitting the net with the ring.
2. Throwing the ring under the net.
3. Relaying the ring or having two teammates touch it in succession.
4. Throwing the ring out of bounds if the opposing team does not touch it.

The team scored upon puts the ring in play again. Five to fifteen points is a game, depending on the skill of the group.

Suggested Use: The ring is used to represent an airplane, and the children's attempts to toss it over the net without allowing it to fall can be compared to *lift.* In attempting to toss the ring over the net, many fouls may be committed, and it should be pointed out that this is due to both the insufficient amount of force of air, the downward pull of gravity and also poor aiming. In most cases more force or lift is needed to launch a ring or plane. When each point is made, it can be referred to as a plane successfully launched. The children might be encouraged to find out how planes are launched from aircraft carriers. They may conclude that a plane must have an enormous lift before it can rise. It can be further pointed out that the force which produces the lift to cause a plane to rise is caused by movements of air, and that this movement produces low pressures over the top of the wings, and high pressures under the bottom of the wings.

Concept: Earth's atmosphere—water cycle.
Activity: Water Cycle Relay

The children are divided into teams of six children each. Each child is assigned a part of the water cycle in the order of the process—that is (1) water vapor, (2) rain, (3) land, (4) stream, (5) river, and (6) ocean. The teams stand in rows close enough to be able to pass a ball from one child to the next. On a signal, the first child of each teams calls his part of the water cycle (water vapor), passes the ball to the second child on his team, and runs to the end of his team's line. The second child calls out his part (rain), passes the ball to the next team member, and moves back in the same manner. This procedure continues until each team has made three complete cycles. The first team to finish wins.

Suggested Use: The cycle is represented by the children moving in turn. As the children pass the ball, it should be emphasized that the various stages are represented by each child. It is important that the children notice the correct order within the cycle and situate themselves in the line accordingly. The ball represents water regardless of the form it takes within the cycle. The game may be adapted by changing the rain part of the cycle to snow or sleet, and by adding brooks and bays if the children so choose.

Conditions of Life

Concept: Variety of life—animals live in many kinds of homes.
Activity: Squirrels in Trees

With the exception of one child, the children are arranged in groups of three around the activity area. Two of the children in each group face each other and hold hands, forming a hollow tree. The third child is a squirrel and stands between the other two children. The extra child who is also a squirrel stands near the center of the activity area. If there is another extra child, there can be two squirrels. The teacher calls, "Squirrel in the tree, listen to me; find yourself another tree!" On the word *tree*, all squirrels must run and get into a different hollow tree, and the extra squirrel also tries to find a tree. There is always one extra squirrel who does not have a tree. At different points in the game, the teacher should have the children change places. The game can then be adapted for other animals such as beavers in dams, foxes or rabbits in holes, bears in caves, and the like.

Suggested Use: In playing this game, children can name other animals and kinds of homes in which they live. They can be encouraged to figure out how they could dramatize the different types of homes animals have, as the two children form the hollow tree.

Concept: Variety of life—animals move about in different ways.
Activity: Animal Relay

The children divide into several teams. The teams stand in rows behind a line about 20 feet from a goal line. The object of the relay is for each team member to move forward to the goal line and return to his place at the rear of his team, moving as quickly as he can according to the type of animal movement assigned. Relays may be varied by the children going to the goal line and back doing imitations of the following animals:

> Donkey Walk—traveling on all fours imitating a donkey's kick.
> Crab Walk—walking on all fours, feet going outside the hands.
> Rabbit Jump—child moves forward bringing his feet forward between his hands.
> Elephant Walk—child bends forward, hands clasped in front with elbows straight and swinging arms like the elephant's trunk.

On a signal, the teams proceed with the relay using the movement indicated by the teacher. The first team finished wins.

Suggested Use: By dramatizing the various movements of animals, children are helped to learn about the differences among animals. Children can be encouraged to figure out ways of moving to represent many types of animals.

Concept: Variety of life—animals escape their enemies in many ways.
Activity: Snail

The children stand in a row with the teacher as the leader at the end of the line. While singing the first verse, the leader walks around in a circle and continues to walk so that the circle becomes smaller. During the singing of the second verse, the leader reverses his direction to enlarge the circle.

> Hand in hand we circle now,
> Like a snail into his shell
> Coming nearer, coming nearer,
> In we go and in we go.
> Aren't you glad this little shell
> Keeps us all and holds us well?
>
> Hand in hand we circle now,
> Like a snail just from its shell
> Going further, going further,
> Out we go and out we go.
> Aren't you glad this little shell
> Kept us all and held us well?

Suggested Use: The concept of animals needing protection from their enemies and employing various means for protection is inherent in this activity. Children might be encouraged to find out other ways animals seek protection from their natural enemies.

Concept: Variety of life—wind is moving air and transports some kinds of seeds.
Activity: Flowers and Wind

The children are divided into two teams, each team having a home marked off at opposite ends of the activity area with a neutral space in between. One team represents a flower, deciding among themselves which flower they shall represent—daisies, lillies, etc. They can then walk over near the home line of the opposite team. The opposing team, representing the wind, stands in a line within their home area ready to run. They guess what the flower chosen by their opponents may be. As soon as the right flower is named, the entire team must turn and run home, the wind chasing them. Any children caught by the wind before reaching home must join the wind team. The remaining flowers repeat their play, taking a different flower name each time. This continues until all of the flowers have been caught. The teams then exchange, and the flower team becomes the wind team.

Suggested Use: In this activity some of the children represent the wind and others represent the flowers and/or seeds. As the flowers walk to the wind home, they represent the flower growing through the summer. When the wind guesses the name of the flower, this represents the end of the growth period. As the flowers begin to run, they represent the seeds, and the children chasing them represent the wind carrying the seeds along. The flowers running also represent the seeds dispersing in different directions being borne by the wind.

Concept: Interdependence of life—some animals live in social groups in which they work together to survive.

Activity: Herds and Flocks

A starting line is drawn. The children are divided into several teams, and stand one behind the other in relay formation at the starting line. A goal line is drawn 30 to 40 feet in front of the starting line. Each member of the relay team is to perform a different action while going to and from the goal line. The teacher assigns the movement to each team member—that is, the first child on each team is to perform one task, the second child on each team is to perform another, etc. Some of the suggested actions are:

> Walk with stiff knees.
> Place hands on hips, hold feet together and jump.
> Proceed in a squat position to goal, run to starting line.
> Hop on one foot.
> Skip to goal, sit down, and skip to starting line.
> Swing arms in circular motion while walking quickly.
> Place hand on head and run.

The signal is given for the first child from each team to proceed with his assigned action. As soon as he returns to the starting line, he touches the extended right hand of the second child on his team, then goes to the end of the line. The second child goes forth performing his designated action. Play continues until one team has had all of its members complete their performances and return to their places. This team is the winner.

Suggested Use: The children can learn in playing this game that, in order to win, all the children must cooperate and perform their different actions in an acceptable manner and as quickly as they can. This can be compared with certain animal groups whose different members perform various tasks for the safety and well-being of the group. The concept can be further integrated into the game by helping children to notice that just as some of the actions in the game are difficult to do, so are some of the things that have to be done in order to survive. The children might be encouraged to find out various roles different members of animal groups perform in order to protect the members of the group from their enemies and to obtain food. They can be helped to identify which type of group member is assigned the different role—that is, the strong to hunt for food, the older for lookouts, etc.

Concept: Interdependence of life—animals have to protect themselves from one another.

Activity: Fox and Sheep

One child is selected to be the fox who stands in his den, a place marked off on one side of the activity area. The rest of the children are the sheep. They stand in the sheepfold, another area marked off on the opposite end of the activity area. The remaining part of the activity area is called the meadows. The fox leaves his den and wanders around the meadow whereupon the sheep sally forth and, approaching the fox, ask him, "Are you hungry, Mr. Fox?" If the fox says, "No, I'm not," the sheep are safe. When the fox says, "Yes, I am!" the sheep must run for the sheepfold as the fox may then begin to chase them. The fox tags as many sheep as he can before they find shelter in the fold. Those sheep who are caught must go to the fox's den and, thereafter, assist the fox in capturing sheep. The original fox is always the first one to leave the den. He is also the one who answers the sheep's questions. The last sheep caught becomes the fox for the next game. This game can be adapted by using other animals who are natural enemies to each other as cat and mouse, hound and rabbit, or fox and geese.

Suggested Use: In this activity the children dramatize the interdependence of animals—that some animals need others for food and are natural enemies. The children can sense the fear of the chase and the need to protect oneself. The children may find out the names of the different types of shelters of the different animals.

Chemical and Physical Changes

Concept: Movement of molecules in solids, liquids and gasses.
Activity: Molecule Ball

The children arrange themselves in a circle. The group then counts off by twos. The number ones face inward, and the number twos face outward—that is, ones and twos are facing each other. Each captain has a ball that is to be moved around the circle until it travels back to the captain. The exact manner in which the balls are to be moved around the circle is determined by the leader calling, "solid, liquid, or gas." When gas is called, the ball is to be thrown from one child to the next; when liquid is called, the ball is to be bounced from one child to the next; and when solid is called, the ball is passed to the next child. When the ball completes the circle, that team which does so first is declared the winner. Whenever a child drops or does not catch the ball passed to him, he must retrieve the ball, return to his place in the circle, then continue to move the ball to the next child.

Suggested Use: The use of solid, liquid, and gas as call words to change the speed of the balls' progress around the circles emphasizes the difference in speed of molecules' movement in solids, liquids, and gasses. The children can be helped to notice that the method of moving the ball around the circle relates to the speed of the movement of molecules in these different states of matter.

Concept: Molecules are in rapid and ceaseless motion.
Activity: Molecule Pass
The class is divided into four groups with each group standing in a straight line. The four groups form a rectangle with each group representing one side of the rectangle. The captain of each group stands near the center of the rectangle in front of his group. On a signal, each captain throws his ball to his group, starting at the right. As each child receives the ball, he throws it back to his captain and assumes a squatting position. When the captain throws the ball to the last child in his group, he runs to the right of his group as the rest of the children stand. The last child on the left runs with the ball to the captain's place, and the procedure is repeated.

Suggested Use: Each ball represents a molecule of matter. The balls are kept in motion at all times. The children can be helped to notice that the ball (the molecule or matter) has to be kept moving. This can lead to a discussion of molecules of different substances, the greater space and rapid movement of molecules of gases (depending on area and temperature) the less rapid movement of molecules of liquids, and the lesser space and least rapid movement of molecules of solids.

Concept: Elements in a compound (the composition of molecules) cannot be separated by physical means.

Activity: Boiling Water

Two or more circles are formed. Each circle is given one or more balls. A container such as a wastebasket is set along the sidelines of the activity area. One child in each circle is the leader. When the teacher calls, "Cold water!" the children in each circle pass the ball from one child to the next. Whenever the teacher calls, "Warm water!" the children roll the ball across the center of the circle from one to another. If the teacher calls, "Boiling water!" the children throw the ball to different ones in the circle. When the teacher calls, "Water vapor!" the ball is immediately thrown to the circle leader who runs with it to the container on the sidelines. The team whose leader reaches the container first wins.

Suggested Use: The ball represents a molecule of water. The ball is one of the surface molecules. At first the molecule moves slowly (cold water). When the water begins to warm up, the speed of the molecule increases (warm water). As the water approaches boiling point, the speed of molecules increases (boiling water). The ball (molecule) has not been altered. It has moved from one place (the liquid state or water) to another place (gaseous state of water vapor).

Concept: Chain reaction comes from one molecule hitting another (or neutrons in radioactive materials).

Activity: Tag and Stoop

The children are scattered over the activity area. One child is *It* and tries to tag two children, one with each hand. When *It* tags the first child, he then grasps the hand of that child. The two continue running after other children until *It* is able to tag a second child. *It* then stands still and gets down in a stooping position. The two children tagged now try to tag two others each, then they stoop down. The four children tagged now continue in the same manner. The object of the game is to see how long it takes for everyone to be tagged.

Suggested Use: In trying to demonstrate chain reaction, the increasingly powerful effect of a small beginning should be brought out. As the children watch the spread of those who are being tagged, they can see this effect.

Concept: Burning is oxidation: the chemical union of a fuel with oxygen.

Activity: Oxygen and Fuel

One child is chosen to be fuel and another child is oxygen. The remaining children join hands and form a circle with fuel in the center of the circle and oxygen on the outside of the circle. The children in the circle try to keep oxygen from getting into the circle and catching fuel. If oxygen gets in the circle, the children in the circle then let fuel out of the circle and try to keep oxygen in, but they must keep their hands joined at all times. When oxygen catches fuel, the game is over, and they join the circle while two other children become fuel and oxygen. If fuel is not caught in a specified period of time, a new oxygen can be selected.

Suggested Use: One child represents the fuel (as trees in a forest), and another, the oxygen (the air). The children in the circle are the preventers of fire. If oxygen catches fuel and ignites him by tagging him, a fire is started. Then the game is over. In this manner the children can be helped to notice that oxygen feeds fire and that oxygen must be kept from fires that have been started in order to put them out. The children might be encouraged to find out ways that fires are smothered depending upon the type of burning material.

Light

Concept: When light strikes a solid object, it bounces.
Activity: Light Bounce
The children are divided into several teams. Two lines are marked on the activity area parallel to a blank wall. One line is drawn six inches from the wall and is the goal line. The second line is drawn 12 feet from the wall. Behind this second line, the teams stand in rows. Each team is given a small wooden block. The first child on each team takes turns throwing his block. If the block lands between the goal line and the wall, a point is scored for that team. If the block falls outside the goal line, each other team gets a point. Each child on the team proceeds in the same manner until each child has had a throw. The team with the highest score wins.

Suggested Use: Children can be helped to notice that the wooden blocks rebound from the wall just as light rays do upon coming in contact with a solid object.

Concept: Heat and light can be reflected.
Activity: Heat and Light
The children are divided into several teams. The teams make rows at a specified distance from the blank wall of a room or the building. The first child on each team throws a ball against the wall and catches it as it

bounces back to him, passes it over his head to the next child on the team, and then moves to the end of the line. The team to complete the procedure first wins.

Suggested Use: Attention can be called to the fact that light and heat are reflected just as the ball hits the wall and bounces back; light and heat are reflected or bounced off by a mirror or other shiny surface.

Concept: A prism can separate a beam of white light into a spectrum.
Activity: Spectrum Relay

The class is divided into two teams so that there will be seven children on each team. Each team forms a row behind a starting line. The children on each team are then assigned a specific color of the spectrum and stand in the correct order that colors appear in the spectrum—red, orange, yellow, green, blue, indigo, and violet. Each child is given the appropriate color tag to pin on his clothing so that his teammates can quickly see where to line up. Those children who are not assigned to a relay team are the prism and stand a given distance away from the starting line; they space themselves several feet apart, facing the relay teams. On a signal, all the children on each team must run between and around back of the children standing a distance away (the prism) and return to the starting line. The team must then join hands so that each team finishes by being lined up in the correct order of colors in the spectrum behind the starting line. The first team lined up correctly behind the starting line wins. A few children may change places with those who did not have a chance to run in the first relay.

Suggested Use: This relay provides children the opportunity to dramatize the concept of the prism. The teams represent the beams of light before passing through the glass prism (represented by the children standing a distance away) and that after they passed through the glass prism, they then represented the band of colors called the *visible spectrum.* During the discussion it can be pointed out that each color of light travels through the glass prism at a different speed. The children can be encouraged to find out about different things in nature that serve as prisms to create visible spectrums.

Energy

Concept: A body left to itself, free from the action of other bodies, will, if at rest, remain at rest.
Activity: Pin Guard

The children form a circle. Ten pins or other suitable objects are set up in the middle of the circle. One child is selected as a guard to protect the pins. On a signal, the children start rolling a ball to knock over the pins. The guard tries to keep the ball away from the pins by kicking it back toward the circle. The child who succeeds in knocking down a pin becomes the new guard.

Suggested Use: The pins in this game represent the body at rest (inertia), and the ball, the force that puts the body in motion. It can be pointed out to the children that the pins in the center of the circle remain at rest until an outside force (the ball) strikes the pins and puts them in motion.

Concept: Friction
Activity: Siamese Twins

The children get in pairs and sit back to back with arms folded and legs extended straight ahead and together. The object is to see which pair can stand first with feet together while maintaining the folded arm position.

Suggested Use: Before the activity the children can talk about some of the results of friction such as heat and the resulting problems confronting scientists who design space missiles. The class might discuss ways in which friction helps them—that is, the friction between feet and ground when one walks and how the use of snow tires or chains provides friction in snow and icy weather. During and after this activity, the teacher can help the children to see how the friction of their feet against the floor keeps them from sliding down. After the activity the children might plan to chart lists of ways in which friction helps them.

Concept: Machines make work easier—arm as lever.
Activity: Hot Potato

The class is divided into even number lines of five or six children each, separated by arm lengths from each other. Each line faces another line five to twenty feet away. Each child has a turn holding a ball at chest height in one hand and hitting it with the palm of the other hand directing the ball to the line facing him. Each child of the opposite line scores one point for each ball he catches. The child who catches the ball then proceeds to hit the ball back to the opposite line who tries to catch the ball to score a point. The child with the highest score wins.

Suggested Use: The use of the arm as a lever can be demonstrated in this activity. The teacher might draw a picture on the chalkboard to show children how the arm works as a lever.

Concept: The lever (in the third-class lever the effort is placed between the load and the fulcrum).

Concept: The greater a force applied to a mass, the greater the acceleration of that mass will be.

Activity: Net Ball (*Note:* Two concepts can be developed by Net Ball)

Before this activity the children can be told that serving is a basic skill used in the game of Net Ball, and for a successful game of Net Ball it is necessary to learn to serve the ball properly. The server stands on the end line facing the net. He holds the ball in his left hand about waist high in front of him and to the right. He hits the ball underhand with his right hand (heel or fist). The weight of the body is transferred forward to the left foot as the right arm moves forward in a follow-through movement. For left-handed children the procedure is reversed.

The children are divided into two groups, each group spaced in a pattern on one side of the net facing the other group. After the teacher demonstrates several times, each child is given the opportunity to attempt to serve the ball two or three times. Following practice, the game is started by one child serving the ball over the net. Any opposing team member may hit the ball with his hands back to the other side of the net. The ball may not be relayed to another child on the same team. Play continues until a point is scored. A point is scored each time the ball hits the surface area in the opponents' court or any of the following violations are committed:

1. Hitting the net with the ball
2. Hitting the ball under the net
3. Relaying the ball or having two teammates touch it in succession
4. Hitting the ball out of bounds if opposing team does not touch it.

Suggested Use: (the lever) During the practice it can be shown how the arm has acted as a lever in the serving action, that the elbow joint was the fulcrum, the forearm was the effort, and the ball was the load. Children can then be encouraged to find other examples that would illustrate this type of lever—a man swinging a golf club or a boy swinging at a ball with a bat.

Suggested Use: (force and acceleration) It can be noted that the servers have difficulty getting the ball in the opposite court, that the ball either fails to go over the net or it is hit out of bounds on the opposite side. The teacher can stop the activity to ask what makes the ball go out of bounds. The children might notice that it was hit too hard. If the ball fails to go over the net, it can be pointed out that it was not hit hard enough. The teacher can then ask the class to explain what factor influences the speed and distance the ball travels. The force of the serve or how hard the ball is hit governs the acceleration of the ball. The children can be encouraged to apply this concept to other types of activities such as batting a baseball, peddling a bicycle or a rocket booster.

Concept: Electricity is the flow of electrons in a closed circuit.
Activity: Electric Ball

The children form a circle and join hands (representing a closed circuit). The children are to move a soccer ball or similar-type ball around the inside of the circle. The ball represents the current or flow of electrons. The children move the ball from one child to the next by using the instep of the foot as in soccer. The object of the game is to keep the ball moving around the circle and preventing the ball from leaving the circle by blocking it with the feet or legs while keeping the hands joined at all times. If the ball leaves the circle (an open or broken circuit), the two children between whom the ball escapes the circle are each given a point. The game continues with the children having the lowest scores as winners.

Suggested Use: Children are able to see this concept demonstrated in this activity, that of the flow of electrons through a closed circuit by passing the ball around the circle and that a broken circuit prevents the flow of electricity when the ball leaves the circle.

Concept: Electricity is the flow of electrons in a closed circuit.
Activity: Current Relay

Children are arranged in teams in rows. Each child reaches back between his legs with his right hand and grasps the left hand of the child immediately in back of him. (Teams should be composed of all boys or all girls). On a signal, the teams thus joined together race to the goal line some 30 or 40 feet from the starting line, then race back to the starting line. The team finishing first with the line unbroken wins.

Suggested Use: The joined hands of the members of the teams represent the closed circuit. As long as the circuit remains unbroken, electricity can flow. (The children can move their feet and proceed with the race.) If the circuit is broken, it has to be repaired (the children rejoin hands) before electricity can continue to flow and the team can move forward again.

Concept: Lightning is electricity.

Activity: Lightning Relay

The class is divided into several teams. The first child on each team toes a starting line. On a signal, he jumps. Someone marks the heel print of each jumper. The next child on each team steps forward to the heel mark of the first child, toes his mark, and jumps. This procedure is continued until every child on each team has jumped. The team having jumped the greatest distance wins.

Suggested Use: Each child is electricity or lightning jumping from one cloud to another. The concept of lightning being electricity gathering in a cloud and jumping to the ground or to another cloud can be noted by the children as they dramatize it in this activity.

Concept: Electricity flows along metal conductors and will not flow along nonmetal conductors as glass or rubber.

Activity: Keep Away

If there is a large number of children, they should form a circle. For a small group, the children may spread out and form a square or five-sided figure. One child is chosen to be *It,* and he stands in the center. The other children throw a ball around the circle or across the square. They try to keep the ball away from *It* while he tries to get his hands on it. If *It* catches the ball he changes places with the last child who threw it, and the game continues. If *It* is unable to get hold of the ball in one minute another *It* can be chosen.

Suggested Use: The ball becomes the electricity, the ball throwers are the conductors, and *It* is a nonconductor who tries to interfere with the flow of electricity. Any time the nonconductor is successful in interfering, the current of electricity is interrupted. Children can be encouraged to find out the kind of materials that are nonconductors and several safety practices that have developed for those working around electricity, both in business and around the home.

Concept: The force of a magnet will pass through many materials.

Activity: Hook On Tag

This activity has been described elsewhere in the book (see p. 90).

Suggested Use: Before starting the game, it should be pointed out that the runner in the game is the magnet. When he is successful in hooking onto the end of one of the groups, the power of the magnet travels through the group to the first person, and he becomes the new magnet. This activity dramatizes that a magnet does not have to be in direct contact with another magnetic material in order to attract it. Later, children can be encouraged to experiment to determine which materials the force of a magnet will travel through.

Concept: Unlike poles of a magnet attract each other.
Activity: North and South

The class is divided into two equal groups. The two groups line up facing each other about 10 feet apart midway between designated goal lines. One group is named north, and the other, south. The teacher has a 10-inch square of cardboard which has an N on one side and an S on the other. The teacher throws the cardboard into the air between the teams where all can see it as it lands. If the S side shows, the south team turns and runs to their goal line, chased by the north team. All who are tagged before reaching the line join north, and the two groups line up facing each other again. The cardboard is thrown into the air again, and the game continues in the same manner. The team which eliminates the other wins.

Suggested Use: The two groups represent the opposite or unlike poles of a magnet, the N and S poles. When one group turns to run to its goal line, it attracts the other group which pursues it.

Concept: Sound carries through the air.
Activity: Stoop Tag

This activity has been described elsewhere in the book (see p. 101).

Suggested Use: After the children have played the game, the teacher can discuss the sound they have heard—singing, shouts, squeels. The teacher can question the children as to how these sounds got to them. It can be pointed out that the sounds were sound waves traveling through the air.

THE SCIENCE MOTOR LEARNING STORY

Early attempts to develop science motor learning stories were patterned after the original procedure used in providing for motor-oriented reading content discussed previously—that is, several stories were written around certain kinds of motor activities, the only difference being that the content also involved reference to science experiences. These stories were tried out in a number of situations. It soon became apparent, as was the case in the mathematics motor learning story, that with some children the development of science concepts in a story was too difficult. The reason for this appeared to be that certain children could not handle both the task of reading while at the same time developing an understanding of the science concept in the story. It was then decided that since *listening* is a first step in learning to read, auditory input should be utilized. This procedure involved having children listen to a story, perform the activity and simultaneously try to develop the science concept that was inherent in the story. When it appeared desirable this process was extended to having the children read the story after having engaged in the activity.

An example of the science motor learning story is one that concerns the game Shadow Tag which is played in the following manner. The players are dispersed over the activity area with one person designated as *It.* If *It* can step on or get into the shadow of another player, that player becomes *It.* A player can keep from being tagged by getting into the shade or by moving in such a way that *It* finds it difficult to step on his shadow. The story about the game is The Shadow Game.

THE SHADOW GAME

Have you ever watched shadows?
When do you see your shadow?
What can your shadow do?
Here is a game to play with shadows.
You can play it with one or more children.
You can be *It.*
Tell your friends to run around, so you cannot step on their shadow.
When you step on a shadow, that child becomes *It.*
You join the other players.
Could you step on someone's shadow?

In one specific situation at first grade level this story was used to introduce the concept *shadows are formed by sun shining on various objects.* Following this a definition of a shadow was given. A discussion led the class to see how shadows are made as well as how they move. The class then went outside the room to the hardtop area where many kinds of shadows were observed. Since each child had a shadow it was decided to put them to use in playing the game.

In evaluating the experience, the teacher felt that the children saw how the sun causes shadows. By playing the game at different times during the day they also observed that the length of the shadow varied with the time of day. It was generalized that the story and the participation in the activity proved very good for illustrating shadows.

All of the practices presented in the book have been carefully researched and extensively field tested with a large number of children, and have been found to be successful when applied in the appropriate manner.

BIBLIOGRAPHY

Annett, M. and Manning, M., Reading and a Balanced Polymorphism for Laterality and Ability, *The Journal of Child Psychology and Psychiatry and Allied Disciplines*, May 1990.

Anshel, M. H., An Information Processing Approach to Teaching Motor Skills, *Journal of Physical Education, Recreation and Dance*, May/June 1990.

Arnold, P. J., The Preeminence of Skill as an Educational Value in the Movement Curriculum, *Quest*, April 1991.

Battinelli, T., Fatigue, Muscular Work and Motor Learning, *The Physical Educator*, Fall 1987.

Beuter, H. and Duda, J. L., Analysis of the Arousal/Motor Performance Relationship in Children Using Movement Kinematics, *Journal of Sports Psychology*, September 1985.

Blackwell, J. R., Time Series Analysis of Knowledge of Results Effects During Motor Skill Acquisition, *Research Quarterly for Exercise and Sports*, March 1991.

Boyce, B. A., Beyond Show and Tell—Teaching the Feel of Movement, *Journal of Physical Education, Recreation and Dance*, January 1991.

Bunker, L. K., The Role of Play and Motor Skill Development in Building Children's Self-confidence and Self-esteem, *The Elementary School Journal*, May 1991.

Chiarenza, G. A., Motor-perceptual Function in Children with Developmental Reading Disorders: Neuropsychophysiological Analysis, *Journal of Learning Disabilities*, June/July 1990.

Council of Learning Disabilities, Measurement and Training of Perceptual and Perceptual-motor Function, *Journal of Learning Disabilities*, June/July 1987.

Densem, J. F., et al., Effectiveness of a Sensory Integrative Therapy Program for Children with Perceptual-motor deficits, *Journal of Learning Disabilities*, April 1989.

Eastman, K. and Safran, J. S., Activities to Develop Your Students' Motor Skills, *Teaching Exceptional Children*, Fall 1986.

Eckhert, H. M., Is There Any New Thinking on the Relationship Between Motor and Intellectual Development? *Journal of Physical Education, Recreation and Dance*, August 1988.

Elliot, M., et al., The Moving Children Project: A Conceptual Process-Oriented Model for Skills Development in Children, *Journal of School Health*, October 1990.

Fry, Prem S. and Lupart, Judy Lee, *Cognitive Processes in Children's Learning: Practical*

191

Applications in Education Practice and Classroom Management, Springfield, IL, Charles C Thomas Publisher, 1987.

Harris, J. C., Usefulness of Motor Learning Research for Physical Education, *Quest,* August 1990.

Horn, E. M., Basic Motor Skill Instruction for Children with Neuromotor Delays: A Critical Review, *Journal of Special Education,* Summer 1991.

Humphrey, James H., *An Overview of Childhood Fitness: Theoretical Perspectives and Scientific Bases,* Springfield, IL, Charles C Thomas Publisher, 1991.

Humphrey, James H., *Integration of Physical Education in the Elementary School Curriculum,* Springfield, IL, Charles C Thomas Publisher, 1990.

Humphrey, James H., *Teaching Children To Relax,* Springfield, IL, Charles C Thomas Publisher, 1988.

Humphrey, James H., *Child Development Through Physical Education,* Springfield, IL, Charles C Thomas Publisher, 1980.

Humphrey, James H., and Humphrey, Joy N., *Developing Elementary School Science Concepts Through Active Games,* 1991.

Humphrey, James H. and Humphrey, Joy N., *Mathematics Can Be Child's Play,* Springfield, IL, Charles C Thomas Publisher, 1990.

Humphrey, James H. and Humphrey, Joy N., *Reading Can Be Child's Play,* Springfield, IL, Charles C Thomas Publisher, 1990.

Humphrey, James H., and Humphrey, Joy N., *Sports Skills for Boys and Girls,* Springfield, IL, Charles C Thomas Publisher 1980.

Humphrey, Joy N., and Humphrey, James H., *Child Developing During the Elementary School Years,* Springfield, IL, Charles C Thomas Publisher, 1989.

Kamen, G. and Morris, H. H., Differences in Sensorimotor Processing of Visual and Proprioceptive Stimuli, *Research Quarterly for Exercise and Sports,* March 1988.

Karp, G. G. and DePauw, K., Neurodevelopment Bases of Human Development, *The Physical Educator,* Spring 1989.

Kelly, Noeline Thompson and Kelly, Brian John, *Physical Education for Pre-school and Primary Grades,* Springfield, IL, Charles C Thomas Publisher, 1985.

McCullagh, P. Model Similarity Effects on Motor Performance, *Journal of Sports Psychology,* September 1987.

Mechling, H., Learning of Movement Skills—Theoretical Considerations for Practical Decisions, *International Journal of Physical Education,* 24, 4, 1987.

Mielke, D. and Morrison, C., Motor Development and Skill Analysis: Connections to Elementary Physical Education, *Journal of Physical Education, Recreation and Dance,* November/December 1985.

Oermann, M. H., Psychomotor Skill Development, *The Journal of Continuing Education in Nursing,* September/October 1990.

Poest, C. A., Challenge Me to Move: Large Muscle Development in Young Children, *Young Children,* July 1990.

Reeve, T. G., Precision of Knowledge of Results: Consideration of the Accuracy Requirements Imposed by the Task, *Research Quarterly for Exercise and Sports,* September 1990.

Rosenbaum, D. A., Successive Approximations to a Model of Human Motor Programming, *The Psychology of Learning and Motivation*, 21, 1987.

Schiller, W. and Schiller, J., Motor Programs in Early Childhood Training: A Preservice Interactive Model, *Early Child Development and Care*, 62, 1990.

Sidaway, B., et al., Summary and Frequency of KR Presentation Effects on Retention of a Motor Skill, *Research Quarterly for Exercise and Sports*, March 1991.

Silvestic, L., The Use of Knowledge of Results in the Acquisition and Performance of Motor Skills, *Education*, Winter 1988.

Sugar, M., Locomotor Development and Oral Reflexes, *Child Psychiatry and Human Development*, Spring 1987.

Thaut, M. H., The Use of Auditory Rhythm and Rhythmic Speech to Aid Temporal Muscular Control in Children with Gross Motor Dysfunction, *The Journal of Music Therapy*, Fall 1985.

Weiss, M. R., "Show and Tell" in the Gymnasium: An Investigation of Developmental Differences in Modeling and Verbal Rehearsal of Motor Skills, *Research Quarterly for Exercise and Sports*, September 1987.

INDEX

195